Name Above All Names Devotional

Focusing on 26 Alphabetical Names of Christ

Beth Willis Miller

Illustrated by Krista Hamrick

Beth Willis Miller with illustrations by Krista Hamrick

Copyright © 2016 Beth Willis Miller
All illustrations Copyright © 2016 Krista Hamrick
All rights reserved.
ISBN: 1523400854
ISBN-13: 978-1523400850

Dedication

Dedicated to my Lord and Savior Jesus Christ and the wonderful family with whom He has blessed me: Jack, Jason, Tracy, Zac, Colton, and Carson.

Contents

	Acknowledgments	1
Chapter 1	Alpha and Omega	3
Chapter 2	Bread of Life	9
Chapter 3	Creator of All Things	13
Chapter 4	Deliverer	21
Chapter 5	Everlasting Father	25
Chapter 6	Friend	29
Chapter 7	Good Shepherd	35
Chapter 8	Healer	39
Chapter 9	Immanuel	43
Chapter 10	Lion of Judah	47
Chapter 11	King of Kings	53
Chapter 12	Light of the World	57
Chapter 13	Bright Morning Star	63
Chapter 14	Name Above All Names	69
Chapter 15	One God	75
Chapter 16	Prince of Peace	79
Chapter 17	Unquenchable Love	85
Chapter 18	Risen Lord	89
Chapter 19	Savior	95
Chapter 20	Truth	101
Chapter 21	Upholder of All Things	107
Chapter 22	The True Vine	113
Chapter 23	Word of Life	117
Chapter 24	Exalted One	123
Chapter 25	Yahweh	127
Chapter 26	King of Zion	133
	About the Author	137
	About the Illustrator	137

Acknowledgments

This beautiful original art print, *Name Above All Names Alphabet*, by Krista Hamrick so inspired author Beth Willis Miller that she wrote this devotional focusing on the 26 alphabetical names of Christ. Each of the illustrations which Krista identified are so special, almost like stained glass windows, as she intricately painted each one with its Scripture reference. Beth's heart was drawn to write a devotional word study based on the Scripture reference. Combining the beauty of Krista's artistic excellence with Beth's devotionals is perfect for individual quiet reflection or small group Bible studies focusing on the Name Above All Names—Jesus Christ—and His attributes and characteristics.

"I am the Alpha and the Omega," says the Lord God, "who is and who was and who is to come, the Almighty."

Alpha and Omega
REVELATION 1:8

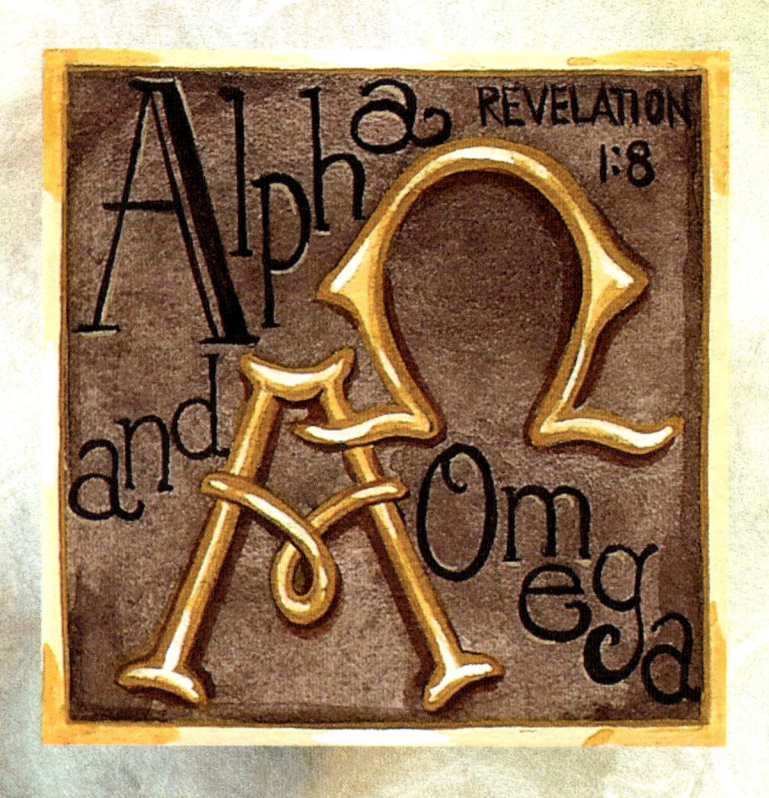

Revelation 1:8

1 Alpha & Omega

Alpha & Omega from Revelation 1:8...

NASB: "I am the Alpha and the Omega," says the Lord God, "who is and who was and who is to come, the Almighty."

Amplified: "I am the Alpha and the Omega [the Beginning and the End]," says the Lord God, "Who is [existing forever] and Who was [continually existing in the past] and Who is to come, the Almighty [the Omnipotent, the Ruler of all]."

Expanded Bible: The Lord God says, "I am the Alpha and the Omega [the first and last letters of the Greek alphabet; 21:6; 22:13]. I am the One who is and [the One who] was and [the One who] is coming [see 1:4]. I am the ·Almighty [All-powerful]."

NLT: "I am the Alpha and the Omega—the beginning and the end," says the Lord God. "I am the one who is, who always was, and who is still to come—the Almighty One."

The Message: The Master declares, "I'm A to Z. I'm The God Who Is, The God Who Was, and The God About to Arrive. I'm the Sovereign-Strong."

Young's Literal: `I am the Alpha and the Omega, beginning and end, saith the Lord, who is, and who was, and who is coming -- the Almighty.'

Pastor Henry Allen "Harry" Ironside has said: "In Revelation 1:8 we read the words of the Son who declared Himself to be Jehovah also, One eternally with the Father. He is the Alpha and Omega—the first and last letters of the Greek alphabet—the beginning and the ending. He created all things; He will wind up all things and bring in the new heavens and the new earth. He is, and was, and is the coming One. He is El Shaddai—the Almighty—who of old appeared to Abraham. May our hearts be occupied with Him and His return be our "blessed Hope!"

Pastor J. Hampton Keathley III writes: "I Am the Alpha and Omega." These are the first and last letters of the Greek alphabet. It is equivalent to our A and Z. This does not relate so much to time but to truth. It expressed the extent of God's knowledge and wisdom (Col. 2:3). It stresses Christ's or the Godhead's omniscience or infinite knowledge and wisdom. This stands then as a strong authentication of the book of Revelation because it comes from the Alpha and Omega. In life, we understand these concepts. Things begin…things end. Jobs start…jobs stop. Decades come…decades go. Birth…death. But there is something special and unique about the words Alpha and Omega as they appear in Revelation 1:8. Jesus Christ used those terms to describe Himself—terms that refer to His deity. When used in Scripture, the words have an almost unfathomable meaning. Jesus, the Alpha, had no beginning. He existed before time, before the creation of the universe. Jesus cannot be limited by the word Alpha. As the Omega, He is not the "end" as we know it. He will continue to exist into the everlasting, never-ending future. It's mind-boggling and awe-inspiring—this view of our Lord. He's the one "who is and who was and who is to come."

Pastor John MacArthur states: In Revelation 1:8, "The Lord God says, 'I am the Alpha and the Omega, who is and who was and who is to come, the Almighty.'" God is saying, if you think this may not happen, I just want to affirm who is in charge of this event and who He is. So, "the Lord God says." The speaker is Jehovah. This, by the way, is His signature on the certainty of the second coming. This is absolutely magnificent. God puts His signature on this prophecy by emphasizing three of His attributes: (1) His omniscience: "I am the Alpha and the Omega." What are "alpha" and "omega"? The first and last letters of the Greek alphabet. Why is God saying, "I am Alpha and Omega?" He is saying, "I am the supreme, sovereign alphabet in which is contained all knowledge." That's what He's saying. "I am alpha to omega, I am A to Z. I contain all knowledge. There is no information, there is no knowledge, there is no truth, there is no understanding, there is no wisdom outside of what I know. When I say Christ is coming, I'm telling you there won't be any surprises because there's nothing outside My knowledge. I am Alpha to Omega. I know everything. And since I have all knowledge, there is nothing I don't know about. There is nothing that exists or could happen to ever foil this plan because there's nothing I don't know about. There are no unknown factors that could sabotage the second coming." (2) His omnipresence: He identifies Himself as the One "who is and who was and who is to come." This is really an astounding statement. He doesn't say, "I am the One who was there, who is here, and who will be over there." He just says, "I was, I am and I will be." And it is open ended. Here God is affirming His eternal presence. He is everywhere at all times. He always has been. He always will be. And He is. His presence is not bounded. His presence is not limited by time or by space. God is saying, "I am everywhere all the time at all times, and so there's nothing outside of where I am. There's nothing that can happen before I'm around and there's nothing that can happen after I leave because there's never a before I'm there and there's never a time when I'm gone. And when I say Jesus is coming, it is settled because all matters, all issues, all persons, all events, all places, and all realities for all eternity are visible to Me." (3) His omnipotence: At the end of Revelation 1:8, He says I'm "the Almighty." He is the supreme power. Yes, He has all knowledge. Yes, He is ever and everywhere present. And yes, He is in absolute, sovereign, complete, control of every single thing. When John says He's coming, He's coming. And God is going to guarantee it. And He's going to come in a glory cloud and the whole world is going to see Him. God guarantees it by His person in Revelation 1:8."

As we look at the state of the world around us, at what has happened in the past and what we may face in the year ahead, there is much to fear: Will a sniper terrorize our community as has happened in other areas? Will the bottom fall out of the economy? Will my job be jeopardized? Will there be violence at my child's school? Fear about possibilities like these can consume us, producing increased stress and even illness. But Revelation 1:8 tells us that there is only one thing to fear—God himself. This fear is not an unhealthy fear that leads to cringing and hiding as Adam and Eve did after they had disobeyed God. Rather, it is a humble and honest recognition of God's beauty, sovereignty, and preeminence so that worshiping and serving him take first place in our lives. It is a healthy reverence that leads to intimacy and an understanding that the power of God residing in us by his Spirit is greater than the power of our fears or of our enemy Satan. A deep sense of awe about who God is leads to the true knowledge and wisdom we desperately need for our lives today and in the year ahead. No matter how out of control things may appear, God's plan remains in place. He is running the show and knows the end from the beginning. No one is higher or mightier than the Lord! He governs our world, his kingdom will come, and his sovereign will shall be done on earth as it is in heaven! God's intentions can never be shaken, and his plans stand firm forever. His amazing power is at work in the world, and he will carry out his eternal purpose to the last detail.

Lord Jesus, thank You that You are the Alpha and the Omega, the beginning and the end, Who is, Who was, and Who is to come, the Almighty. Develop in me a deep reverence of You that leads to life, wisdom, and greater intimacy with You. Open my heart to be teachable and to receive correction and discipline willingly. Grant that I would fear You, and not my circumstances in the present or the what-ifs of the future. May I be so filled with Your love that faith would replace my fear. Let it be forever settled in my heart that You are returning. Help me to share Your life with others who yearn to know more about You. Open my eyes to the signs that are all around me so that I might prepare for and anticipate Your return. Because You have all authority on earth and in heaven, I can rest in You. You are God, without beginning or end. I am thankful that wherever I go, I don't have to feel insecure or anxious because you are there! Thank You for Your faithfulness and loving-kindness that follows me all the days of my life. Help me to trust You, knowing that You are in control and that You are using everything that happens in my life to show me that in You I am complete and lack nothing. In Jesus' mighty Name Above All Names--Alpha and Omega, we pray, amen.

Look Up—meditate on Revelation 1:8

Look In—as you meditate on Revelation 1:8 pray to see how you might apply it to your life.

Look Out—as you meditate on Revelation 1:8 pray to see how you might apply it to your relationships with others.

Notes

I am the bread of life.
I am the living bread
which came down
out of heaven.
If anyone eats
of this bread,
he will live forever.

Bread of Life

JOHN 6:48

John 6:48, 51

2 Bread of Life

Bread of Life from John 6:48…

NASB: I am the bread of life.

Amplified: I am the Bread of Life [the Living Bread which gives and sustains life].

Expanded Bible: I am the ·bread that gives life [bread of life].

Living Bible: Yes, I am the Bread of Life!

The Voice: I am the bread that gives life.

Bread was the primary food of people in Bible times. It was made from a variety of grains, often mixed with lentils or beans. The "loaves" were baked flat, about a half inch thick. In the Bible, bread is symbolic as the sustainer of physical life.

Theologian Haddon W. Robinson writes: "Years ago my wife and I took our children to an amusement park in Texas. By day's end, Vicki and Torrey were tired and hungry. As we were leaving, we passed a concession stand and Vicki asked for some cotton candy. I told her we would get some real food in a few minutes, but she wouldn't hear of it. So I decided to invest $1.50 to teach her a lesson. Vicki got the cotton candy she begged for. But as she bit into it, she discovered there was nothing to it. Finally she handed it back to me and said, "Daddy, it's not real!" She knew she was hungry, and she learned that cotton candy promises something it can't deliver. There is a deep hunger within all of us. Sigmund Freud believed people are hungry for love. Karl Jung insisted that we crave security. Alfred Adler maintained that significance is what we are after. But Jesus declared, "I am the bread of life" John 6:48. Jesus was saying that if we want the deepest hunger of our life satisfied, we need to go to Him to be filled. He knew that our hunger and thirst are really for Him. Don't settle for spiritual cotton candy when Christ can fill the emptiness in your life. Only the Bread of Life can satisfy our spiritual hunger."

Pastor John MacArthur states: "I want to draw your attention to John 6:32-59 where our Lord gives this great sermon on, I Am the Bread of Life. He repeats that several times. "I am the Bread of Life." It is interesting to note also that the word "Bethlehem" in Hebrew means "house of bread." This sermon is a shocking day toward the end of the Galilean ministry of Jesus as He taught the Jewish people in the synagogue at Capernaum. The most compelling statement around which all of this is built is the repeated statement, "I am the Bread of life." That's His claim, verse 32, verse 33, verse 48. This is the first of seven "I AMs" in the Gospel of John, in which our Lord takes the verb "to be" in Hebrew, the name of God who is the "I AM that I AM," and applies it to Himself and adds a metaphor. "I am the Bread of life. I am the Good Shepherd. I am the Vine. I am the Way. I am the Truth. I am the Life. I am the Resurrection and the Life." All of those I AMs are efforts on the part of our Lord to make clear that He is one in the same as God. This is the first of those seven I AMs, in which He takes the name of God, and in this case applies as He does on several of those occasions, a metaphor to explain something about His nature and His work. Now, you have to understand how monumental this sermon was given in the Capernaum synagogue. He's talking to Jewish people, and He presents this powerful claim that He has come down from heaven. Jesus is saying, "I AM the means by which eternal life can become yours." To say that He is bread is to use really a metonym for food, nourishing food that gives life and sustenance. Bread, then, was simply a word that encompassed all nutritious food. Jesus is saying that, "I am your food. I am your true soul food." Eating is necessary. Eating is in response to hunger. Eating is personal and eating is transformational. If you don't eat physically, you will die. If you eat, the food you take in transforms you, and that's what Christ does. We are praying for those who have come, looked, or are looking, but haven't believed, received, eaten, accepting Christ, not only as the bread that nourishes the soul, but the blood that cleanses the soul."

Jesus is the Bread of Life, the Light of the World, our Counselor, our Good Shepherd. Prayerfully studying and meditating on the character traits and names of God is one of the most faith-building, encouraging things you can do for your spiritual life. It will dispel your anxiety and boost your faith. It will enable you to trust God more. Knowing the true character of God will renew and transform your mind with the truth, dissolve doubt, and breathe life into your soul. Saying aloud the attributes of the Lord and thinking about how you've experienced different aspects of His character can be a powerful act of worship. Ask God to reveal Himself to you in greater clarity than you've ever experienced before.

Lord Jesus, my Bread of Life, thank You that You have put within each of us a spiritual hunger that only You can fill. Cause me to hunger and thirst for You and Your life today. I want to join You in what You are doing to rescue those who are perishing, to feed those who are hungry and thirsty with your Bread of Life and Living Water. Help me to hear and obey when You call on me. Empower me to be Your hands and Your feet in the place where I live. In Jesus' mighty Name Above All Names—Bread of Life, we pray, amen.

Look Up—meditate on John 6:48

Look In—as you meditate on John 6:48 pray to see how you might apply it to your life.

Look Out—as you meditate on John 6:48 pray to see how you might apply it to your relationships with others.

For by Him all things
were created
in the heavens
and on the earth,
visible things
and
invisible things.

COLOSSIANS 1:16

Creator of all things

Colossians 1:16

3 Creator of All Things

Creator of All Things from Colossians 1:16…

NASB For by Him all things were created, both in the heavens and on earth, visible and invisible, whether thrones or dominions or rulers or authorities—all things have been created through Him and for Him.

Amplified: For it was in Him that all things were created, in heaven and on earth, things seen and things unseen, whether thrones, dominions, rulers, or authorities; all things were created and exist through Him [by His service, intervention] and in and for Him.

Lightfoot: For in and through him the whole world was created, things in heaven and things on earth, things visible to the outward eye and things cognizable by the inward perception. His supremacy is absolute and universal. All powers in heaven and earth are subject to him. This subjection extends even to the most exalted and most potent of angelic beings, whether they are called thrones or dominations or princedoms or powers, or whatever title of dignity men may confer on them. Yes: he is the first and he is the last. Through him, as the mediatorial Word, the universe has been created; and unto him, as the final goal, it is tending. In him is no before or after. He is preexistent and self-existent before all the worlds.

Phillips: He existed before creation began, for it was through him that everything was made, whether spiritual or material, seen or unseen. Through him, and for him, also, were created power and dominion, ownership and authority. In fact, every single thing was created through, and for him.

Wuest: because in Him were created all things in the heavens and upon the earth, the visible things and the invisible ones, whether they are thrones or lordships or principalities or authorities. All things through Him as intermediate agent and with a view to Him stand created. |

Young's Literal: because in him were the all things created, those in the heavens, and those upon the earth, those visible, and those invisible, whether thrones, whether lordships, whether principalities, whether authorities; all things through him, and for him, have been created.

By Him all things were created. All things means just that—all things. Even the hill called Golgotha. Even the thorns that pierced His blessed brow. Even the Cross that brought His agonizing death. How great is His love for His creation that He would die for it to redeem it!

By Him (en) is literally "in Him", the preposition "in" (Greek = en) denoting that Christ is the sphere within which the work of creation takes place. All the laws and purposes which guide the creation and government of the universe reside in Him. ""By Him" is en autōi, here, not instrumental but locative; "in Him" were all things created." (Wuest)

Theologian William E. Vine writes: "In Him" describes Him as the Designer, the One Who, in fellowship with the Father, determined the condition of all things and the laws which govern and control them."

Theologian John Eadie writes: "by (in) Him"—We rather hold "that the act of creation rests in Christ originally, and its completion is grounded in Him." He is not simply instrumental cause, but He is also primary cause. The impulse to create came upon Him from no co-ordinate power of which He was either the conscious or the passive organ. All things were created in Him—the source of motive, desire, and energy was in Him. He was not, as a builder, working out the plans of an architect—but the design is His own conception, and the execution is His own unaided enterprise. He did not need to go beyond Himself, either to find space on which to lay the foundation of the fabric, or to receive assistance in its erection."

Theologian Charles F. Moule explains: "In other words, the mighty fact that all things were created was bound up with Him, as its Secret. The creation of things was in Him, as the effect is in its cause."

Pastor Marvin Vincent says: "In is not instrumental but local; not denying the instrumentality, but putting the fact of creation with reference to its sphere and center. In Him, within the sphere of His personality, resides the Creative will and the creative energy, and in that sphere the creative act takes place. Thus creation is dependent on Him. The (definite) article (ta panta = "the things") gives the collective sense—the all, the whole universe of things. Without the article it would be all things severally." Note the emphatic repetition of "all things" which would include the seen and the unseen world! The universe of things, not all things severally, but "all things collectively." The phrase literally reads "the all things." Seven times in six verses Paul mentions "all creation," "all things" and "everything," thus stressing that Christ is supreme over all."

Were created (ktizo) in the New Testament is always used of an act of God creating something out of nothing. Paul affirms that creation was a real event in time! Were created is the aorist tense, which points to the definite historical act of creation.

Theologian Charles F. Moule writes: "The Greek verb ktizo denotes the making, constituting, of a new state of things. As a Divine operation, such "creation" is the ordering by sovereign will of the material (of whatever kind) which by that will exists."

Theologian John Eadie writes: "The aorist tense characterizes creation as a past and perfect work. Creation is here in the fullest and most unqualified sense ascribed to Christ, and the doctrine is in perfect harmony with the theology of the beloved disciple. The work of the six days displayed vast creative energy, but it was to a great extent the in bringing of furniture and population to a planet already made and in diurnal revolution, for it comprehended the formation of a balanced atmosphere, the enclosure of the ocean within proper limits, the clothing of the soil with verdure, shrubs, trees, and cereal grasses—the exhibition of sun, moon, and stars, as lights in the firmament—the introduction of bird, beast, reptile, and fish, into their appropriate haunts and elements—and the organization and endowment of man, with Eden for his heritage, and the world for his home. But this demiurgical process implied the previous exercise of Divine omnipotence, for "in the beginning God created the heaven and the earth." It is not, therefore, the wise and tasteful arrangement of pre-existent materials or the reduction of chaos to order, beauty, and life, which is here ascribed to Jesus, but the summoning of universal nature into original existence. What had no being before was brought into being by Him. The universe was not till He commanded it to be. "He spake and it was done." Every form of matter and life owes its origin to the Son of God, no matter in what sphere it may be found, or with what qualities it may be invested. In heaven or on earth—Christ's creative work was no local or limited operation; it was not bounded by this little orb; its sweep surrounds the universe which is named in Jewish diction and according to a natural division—"heaven and earth." Every form and kind of matter, simple or complex—the atom and the star, the sun and the clod—every grade of life from the worm to the angel—every order of intellect and being around and above us, the splendors of heaven and the nearer phenomena of earth, are the product of the First-born."

Theologian H. Wayne House writes: "Christ's creative work was all encompassing, for it includes all created things "in heaven and on earth, visible and invisible." These inclusive qualifiers are significant in light of the problems facing the Colossian church. The entire physical creation, which was distasteful to the incipient Gnostics and ascetics, nevertheless had its origin in Christ. The Incarnation, in which God was manifest in the flesh, was abhorrent enough. But the concept of Christ's having been so closely involved with the physical world as its very Creator was especially repulsive to the heretics. On the other hand Paul affirmed in Colossians that the creation is good, not evil. In contrast to the practice of giving homage to mediatorial heavenly beings, which prevailed in Hellenistic cults and Jewish mysticism, Paul boldly affirmed that everything "invisible"—including angels—is part of the creation that is in Christ, that is, is contained in Him and by Him. This clearly removes them from any position worthy of worship. The first "created" in this verse is aorist tense and in this section the verb is perfect tense, indicating that all things were created at a point in time in the past and that they "stand created" or "remain created." The perfect tense then speaks of the permanence of the universe, the cause of which rests on Christ far more than on gravity! All creation is a Christo-centric universe! "Entropy" in a spiritual sense is devolution from our Creator Christ Jesus. How tragic is this truth! How great the deception that we are evolving toward higher beings. How powerful is the Lie. Believers will all be changed, but that is not evolution but glorification and it transpires in a moment!"

Theologian John Eadie writes: The aorist tense carries us back to the act of creation, which had all its elements in Him, and the perfect tense exhibits the universe as still remaining the monument and proof of His creative might. The first clause depicts creation in its origin, and the second refers to it as an existing effect. In the former, it is an act embodying plan and power, which are alike "in Him"—in the latter, it is a phenomenon caused and still continued "by Him."

By Him is more literally "through Him," the preposition through (dia ~ by means of) with the genitive indicating that Christ is the immediate instrument of creation. "For Him" is literally "unto Him" where the preposition "for" (eis) indicates that Christ is the goal of creation.

Pastor Marvin Vincent writes: "All things came to pass within the sphere of

His personality and as dependent upon it. All things, as they had their beginning in Him, tend to Him as their consummation, to depend on and serve Him."

Pastor Warren W. Wiersbe writes: "Everything exists in Him, for Him, and through Him. Jesus Christ is the Sphere in which they exist, the Agent through which they came into being, and the One for whom they were made. Paul's use of three different prepositions is one way of refuting the philosophy of the false teachers. For centuries, the Greek philosophers had taught that everything needed a primary cause, an instrumental cause, and a final cause. The primary cause is the plan, the instrumental cause the power, and the final cause the purpose. When it comes to Creation, Jesus Christ is the primary cause (He planned it), the instrumental cause (He produced it), and the final cause (He did it for His own pleasure)." Paul repeats that Jesus was the agent of creation and adds that He is the purpose of it as well! The whole of the cosmos was made for Christ! Not only were we created for Him, through His redemption discussed earlier we have in a sense been "re-created" for Him."

Spend time contemplating the awesome majesty and splendor of our Creator and sustainer of the universe, Who has spared nothing to reveal His Father's heart. Recommit yourself to Him and to living according to His ways. Ask for the empowering of his Spirit to delight in doing what God commands. In prayer, lift your voice in extravagant worship of our Lord Jesus Christ, singing praises to His name. Worship Him because He is the perfect, holy, almighty Creator and king of the universe and yet calls you into intimate relationship with Him. Jesus has opened the way for us to experience communion and harmony with our Creator. This is what we were made for! The majesty and brilliance of our God fills the earth. The glory of God is higher than the heavens. Even children and infants give him praise. He set the sky, the moon and the stars, and all the galaxies in place. He is truly an awesome God! From the time we were conceived and born into this world to the very end of our lives, our Creator, who knitted us together in our mother's womb, the same eternal, unchanging One who created the heavens and the earth, is the One who has been caring for us all along, through the hands of parents and others who have loved, nurtured, and taught us. And it is He who will sustain us—throughout our childhood and youth, in our active years of working or parenting, and into the elder years when our hair is white with age and we can no longer care for ourselves but are dependent on the care of others. Our Creator, our Heavenly Father is our God of everlasting care.

Lord Jesus, help me to realize that You are everlastingly my Father, intimately acquainted with me and with every moment of my entire lifetime. Help me to rely on You through every season of my life and to rest in the knowledge that even when I am old, You will still be caring for me. Grant me the grace to enter into true praise and to experience Your delight in me. I want to be lost in wonder, love, and praise. I want to sing songs that lift Your name high. Give me fresh revelation today, Lord, of who you are. Inspire me so that I will sing of your greatness and glory forever! You are the king over all the earth. I love you, Lord. We praise You for who You are. Your glory is higher than the heavens. Your majesty fills the earth. We worship and adore You. Help us to walk as Your children, giving honor and glory to you and never losing sight of Your power or Your love. In Jesus' mighty Name Above All Names—Creator, we pray, amen.

Look Up—meditate on Colossians 1:16

Look In—as you meditate on Colossians 1:16 pray to see how you might apply it to your life.

Look Out—as you meditate on Colossians 1:16 pray to see how you might apply it to your relationships with others.

Notes

He delivered us out of the power of darkness, and transferred us into the Kingdom of the Son of His love; in whom we have our redemption, the forgiveness of our sins.

Deliverer
COLOSSIANS 1:13

Colossians 1:13,14

4 Deliverer

Deliverer from Colossians 1:13...

NASB: For He rescued us from the domain of darkness, and transferred us to the kingdom of His beloved Son,

Amplified: [The Father] has delivered and drawn us to Himself out of the control and the dominion of darkness and has transferred us into the kingdom of the Son of His love.

Lightfoot: Yes, by a strong arm he rescued us from the lawless tyranny of darkness, removed us from the land of our bondage, and settled us as free citizens in our new and glorious home, where his Son, the offspring and the representative of his love, is King;

NLT: For he has rescued us from the one who rules in the kingdom of darkness, and he has brought us into the Kingdom of his dear Son.

Phillips: For we must never forget that he rescued us from the power of darkness, and re-established us in the kingdom of his beloved Son, that is, in the kingdom of light.

Wuest: who delivered us out of the tyrannical rule of the darkness and transferred us into the kingdom of the Son of His love, in whom we are having our liberation, procured by the payment of ransom.

Young's Literal: who did rescue us out of the authority of the darkness, and did translate us into the reign of the Son of His love.

Delivered is the Greek word, *rhuomai* which means to draw or snatch to oneself and invariably refers to a snatching from danger, evil or an enemy. This basic idea is that of bringing someone out of severe and acute danger, and so to save, rescue, deliver, preserve. *Rhuomai* emphasizes greatness of peril from which deliverance is given by a mighty act of power. In the New Testament rhuomai is always associated with God as the Deliverer and with a person as the object of His deliverance.

Rhuomai means to rescue, deliver, as when we first became believers and the Lord...delivered *(rhuomai)* us from the domain of darkness and transferred (removed us from. one place to another, causing a change in someone's official position) us to the kingdom (denoting sovereignty, royal power, dominion) of His beloved Son. Since rhuomai means to draw to oneself, here we see the great picture that God drew us out of Satan's kingdom to Himself. That event was the new birth. We are not gradually, progressively delivered from Satan's power. When we placed our faith in Christ, we were instantly delivered.

A great example is wading in a rushing river and suddenly being caught in the current utterly helpless. As you cry out someone hears you and holds out their hand as you go rushing by. As you lie their beside the river safe in the presence of the one who pulled you out, you still are in the presence of the dangerous rushing current...you can hear it...you can see it...but you've been delivered from danger you are now safe. How foolish to walk right back into that current and let it sweep you away!

Rhuomai is in the present tense indicating that is our Savior continually delivers us. The middle voice is reflexive ("He Himself rescues us") and emphasize His personal involvement in the rescue. He initiates and participates in the carrying out of the rescue. *Rhuomai* is in the aorist tense (past completed act) and the middle voice which conveys the great truth that God initiated the "rescue operation" and participated in the carrying out of the operation! One could paraphrase this verse as "God Himself rescued us" or the Amplified Version's "[The Father] has delivered and drawn us to Himself." This deliverance points to the moment of salvation for every believer—He "rescued" us from sin and death when He died in our place, and that "credit" was placed on our account the moment we first believed this Good News. The truth to depraved men and women is that we did not (and could not) rescue ourselves from the jaws of eternal destruction. God did only what He could do...truly all is grace.

Wing-walker Lee Oman slipped from his perch underneath a Waco biplane and dangled from a safety line 1500 feet over the Hillsboro, Oregon, airport during an air show. At first, everyone in the crowd of 40,000 thought the fall was part of Oman's daring midair act. But after the plane had circled the airport for 20 minutes, it was obvious something had gone wrong. Oman had fallen and didn't have the strength to pull himself back up. When they saw what was happening, several men jumped into a pickup truck and sped onto the runway. The pilot of the biplane saw the truck and realized what the would-be rescuers had in mind. He gently lowered his dangling human cargo over the vehicle until Oman was within reach. While one man grabbed Oman and pulled him into the truck bed, another cut the wing-walker's nylon safety harness. Oman was free of the plane's deadly grasp.

Captain Scott O'Grady knows better than most what rescue means. In June 1995 his plane was shot down over Bosnia. The Air Force pilot survived on insects, plants, and rain water and was only able to use his radio transmitter late at night. On the sixth night of his ordeal, his faint radio signal was picked up by another U.S. pilot. A daring rescue mission eventually brought the helpless pilot to safety. As amazing as this rescue was, every believer has experienced one even more miraculous.

We humans just naturally tend to be self-absorbed, so it is easy to get things all turned around and think that the Christian life is all about me—all about my disciplines and my effort, all about my problems and what I can do to solve them. But this scripture is one that pulls us back to the center, back to the truth: it's all about what God has done--Christ's finished work on the cross--our Deliverer!

Heavenly Father, my Deliverer, I don't know what is going to happen in the next twenty-four hours, but I know that you will give me the strength I need to handle it and to deal with whatever challenges I may face. I bless you, Lord! Give me your peace as I look to you for everything I need. I rejoice in my relationship with You, Father—all because of what Jesus Christ has done for me. Having an intimate relationship with Jesus, the friend of sinners, allows me to have an eternal perspective about everything else that happens to me today. I praise you for the joy such a friendship brings. In Jesus' mighty Name Above All Names—Deliverer we pray, amen.

Look Up—meditate on Colossians 1:13

Look In—as you meditate on Colossians 1:13 pray to see how you might apply it to your life.

Look Out—as you meditate on Colossians 1:13 pray to see how you might apply it to your relationships with others.

His name will be called Wonderful, Counselor Mighty God, Everlasting Father, Prince of Peace.

Everlasting Father
ISAIAH 9:6

Isaiah 9:6

5 Everlasting Father

Everlasting Father from Isaiah 9:6...

NIV: For to us a child is born, to us a son is given, and the government will be on his shoulders. And he will be called Wonderful Counselor, Mighty God, Everlasting Father, Prince of Peace.

Amplified: For to us a Child is born, to us a Son is given; and the government shall be upon His shoulder, and His name shall be called Wonderful Counselor, Mighty God, Everlasting Father [of Eternity], Prince of Peace.

Expanded Bible: A child ·has been [or will be; the prophet views the future as though it had already happened] born to us;·God has given a son [L a son has been given] to us. He will be responsible for leading the people [L The government/rule/dominion will be on his shoulder]. His name will be Wonderful Counselor [or Wonderful! Counselor!; or Extraordinary Advisor], Powerful [Mighty] God, Father Who Lives Forever [Eternal Father], Prince of Peace.

NET: For a child has been born to us, a son has been given to us. He shoulders responsibility and is called: Extraordinary Strategist, Mighty God, Everlasting Father, Prince of Peace.

Eternal Father (in Hebrew is *Abi'ad* [*ab* = father and *ad* = eternal] which literally means "The Father of Eternity") In context, the Son Who is the King functions as a father would over his children—He acts like a father—He protects them, He feels affection and compassion for His children.

Theologian Edward J. Young commenting on Eternal Father writes: "He is One who eternally is a Father to His people. Now and forever He guards His people and supplies their needs. "I am the good shepherd," said our Lord, and thus expressed the very heart of the meaning of this phrase. What tenderness, love, and comfort are here! Eternally—a Father to His people!"

Pastor Harry Ironside writes: "It is easy to get sidetracked when we talk about Jesus as the "Everlasting Father." How can the Son be the Father? As soon as you ask that question you step into the minefield that we like to call the doctrine of the Trinity. Scripture affirms that there is one God who is manifest in three distinct and separate "persons" or personalities: Father, Son and Holy Spirit. The Father is not the Son, the Son is not the Spirit and the Spirit is not the Father. But they are all one God! Jesus is not called Everlasting Father because there is confusion about the nature of God the Father and God the Son. Jesus is called the Everlasting Father because of His father-like qualities. He is still God the Son, but His love and grace is like that of a Father with his children."

Pastor Charles Spurgeon writes: "How complex is the person of our Lord Jesus Christ! Almost in the same breath the prophet calls him a "child," and a "counsellor," a "son," and "the everlasting Father." This is no contradiction, and to us scarcely a paradox, but it is a mighty marvel that he who was an infant should at the same time be infinite, he who was the Man of Sorrows should also be God over all, blessed forever; and that he who is in the Divine Trinity always called the Son, should nevertheless be correctly called "the everlasting Father." How forcibly this should remind us of the necessity of carefully studying and rightly understanding the person of our Lord Jesus Christ! We must not suppose that we shall understand him at a glance. A look will save the soul, but patient meditation alone can fill the mind with the knowledge of the Savior. Glorious mysteries are hidden in his person. He speaks to us in plainest language, and he manifests himself openly in our midst, but yet in his person itself there is a height and depth which human intellect fails to measure."

Jesus is our Everlasting Father in the sense that He is the one who brings us to spiritual life. In John 14:6 Jesus told us that "no man comes to the Father, except through Him." We are new creatures in and because of Christ. It is because of Jesus that we have the opportunity to know eternal life. It is because of Jesus that we can know a new and life-giving relationship with the Father.

As an Everlasting Father, our Lord provides for us. The apostle Paul wrote,

"And my God will meet all your needs according to his glorious riches in Christ Jesus." Knowing that Jesus is the Everlasting Father, shows us that he is not only able to meet these needs, He is also willing to meet them. Our Everlasting Father provides for our every need.

Do you need to feel God's everlasting arms carrying you today because your strength is exhausted? Do you know someone who is in desperate straits and needs God's help? From the time we were conceived and born into this world to the very end of our lives, our Everlasting Father, who knitted us together in our mother's womb, the same eternal, unchanging One who created the heavens and the earth, is the One who has been caring for us all along, through the hands of parents and others who have loved, nurtured, and taught us. It is He who will sustain us—throughout our childhood and youth, in our active years of working or parenting, and into the elder years when our hair is white with age and we can no longer care for ourselves but are dependent on the care of others. Our Everlasting Father is our God of everlasting care.

Everlasting Father, I do want my problems solved and my troubles removed, but from the crushing weight of my burdens, I turn my eyes to You. Enable me to find my rest in You, to discover a place of deeper abandonment and security in Your everlasting love. You are my only rock. You are my only rest. Help me to realize that You are everlastingly my Father, intimately acquainted with me and with every moment of my entire lifetime. Help me to rely on You through every season of my life and to rest in the knowledge that even when I am old, you will still be caring for me. In Jesus' mighty Name Above All Names—Everlasting Father, we pray, amen.

Look Up—meditate on Isaiah 9:6

Look In—as you meditate on Isaiah 9:6 pray to see how you might apply it to your life.

Look Out—as you meditate on Isaiah 9:6 pray to see how you might apply it to your relationships with others.

Greater love has no one than this, that someone lay down his life for his friends.

Friend
JOHN 15:13

John 15:13

6 Friend

Friend from John 15:13 …

NASB: Greater love has no one than this, that one lay down his life for his friends.

Amplified: No one has greater love [no one has shown stronger affection] than to lay down (give up) his own life for his friends.

Expanded: The greatest love a person can show is to die for his friends [No one has greater love than this: to lay down one's life for one's friends; Jesus' death is the ultimate expression of this principle].

J. B. Phillips: There is no greater love than this—that a man should lay down his life for his friends.

Living Bible: And here is how to measure it—the greatest love is shown when a person lays down his life for his friends;

Pastor John MacArthur writes: "As Christians, when we talk about something like friendship with Jesus, when we speak about something that intimate, it's absolutely thrilling to realize that the Son of God, who is responsible for the creation and the upholding of the Universe, is literally a personal intimate friend of those who are his own. It's an overwhelming thing when you really grasp that truth…what it means is to really be a friend of Jesus

Christ. Friendship with Jesus Christ is intimacy with God. "Greater love hath no man than this, that a man lay down his life for his friends." Jesus says, "I want you to love as I loved you." Now you say, well, I can't love in a substitutionary way. That's right; you can't. But you don't have to put too much into this verse. You can't love to a point of redeeming the whole world, we know that. And you can't love with the pure undefiled total agape that Christ can love with, but you can love in character as he loves, and that is, you can love with a sacrificial giving kind of love, and that's what he's saying. He's not expecting you to love in an eternal divine dimension of love equal to Christ. He is expecting you to love as Christ loves. And how does he love? He loves with a sacrificial, self-giving, kind of love. The disciples are not merely to attach themselves to one another externally and be devoted and helpful to each other. They are to agape. They are to love like Jesus loved. They are to love with total self-giving. You are to look at your brother in Christ, not as somebody who's to be kind of your external acquaintance, not some kind of a superficial relationship. You're to look at your brother in Christ and to see him like Jesus would see him. You're to see him in terms of his soul's need. You're to see him in terms of eternal interests. You're to see him in terms of what is his deep heart cry and the anguish of his soul. You're to see him in terms of a self-giving, comforting, spiritually instructing, and burdening-bearing kind of love. And I think sometimes, we substitute this kind of superficial, very much superficial, really on the surface, relationship, for something that is deep and that is really soul-to-soul love, where we care about the intimate needs of the man and the woman who is around us, who is our brother in Christ. And our love like that is going to be our testimony."

Pastor MacArthur continues: "Greater love hath no man than this, that a man lay down his life for his friends." The world over, for all of history, the world has always acknowledged the supreme evidence of love, is when a person would die for the one he loved. And that's exactly what Jesus is about to do. He loves these disciples. If he doesn't die, they'll spend forever in hell, and so would you and so would I and so would everybody else, who ever lived, because there would be no sacrifice for sin. Jesus knows his death is only a few hours away. He's not dying for himself. He bore our sins in his own body on the tree. He became sin for us, He who knew no sin, that we might be made the righteousness of God in Him. He was dying a substitutionary death, and we are the beneficiaries. We're not just witnesses of Calvary. We're the recipients of what was accomplished there. We reap the benefits of his life and his free surrender in death."

The story is told of the mother who loved her child, in Scotland in the highland country, and was taking the baby from one place to another and a snowstorm came. The baby was cold and the mother took off all of her clothes to keep the baby warm, tucked the baby in a place by a tree and naked the mother died. They found her frozen the next day and the baby was warm and alive.

Charles Dickens, in his classic, The Tale of Two Cities, records for us the story of Charles Darney, who caught up in the swirl of the French Revolution, was innocently found guilty. He was really blameless and it was unjust. He was put into prison to await the guillotine. He had a friend, Sidney Carton, who came to the prison, drugged him, took his clothes and because he was so close resembling Darney, took the guillotine for him the next morning, while friends took the 'body' of Darney out. His life was spared because his friend died for him.

Pastor Ray Stedman writes: "Greater love has no one than this, that he lay down his life for his friends." Love lays down its life for another. We all know how fully Jesus Himself exemplified this. His is the greatest love that anyone can demonstrate toward friends. Obviously, this means more than simply dying physically for them. If it meant only that, there would be very few of us who could or would ever fulfill this, largely because we would lack the opportunity to do so. And, of course, one could do so only once! But our Lord is commanding us to do this repeatedly. So He means by this that we are to give ourselves up for one another. When you go out of your way to meet a friend's need, when you are willing to spend time with someone who is a Christian just because that one is a Christian--not necessarily because you are drawn to that person--and you are willing to go out of your way and to give yourself up for him or her, you are laying down your life, a part of it at least, for that person. This is what Jesus had in mind."

There are times when we may feel as if a vast distance separates us from God. There are moments, even days, when it seems as if we are standing outside, watching as others embrace spiritual intimacy with God. Yet the good news is that we don't need to find a special place to share our hearts or use special words to communicate our thoughts, needs, even our fears to God. Our sacred place of meeting is as close as a whisper because Christ lives in us. He invites you to come freely to Him and to sit in His presence, talk with Him as you would with a friend, and continue that dialogue as you work, live, and walk through your day.

Lord Jesus, thank You for being my Friend. It is when I am in Your presence that You reveal Your love for me. In those quiet moments, I can express my thoughts, fears, and longings to walk with You through joyous times and times when I am in the valley of the shadow of death. I am so thankful that You are as close as my heartbeat. Thank You for the privilege of daily being able to meet with You. Thank You for the free gift of salvation, that we are justified on the basis of the finished work of Jesus Christ on the Cross. Thank You that, right now, we are under the completely sufficient imputed righteousness of Christ. Because we have placed our trust in the finished work of Jesus Christ, we are redeemed by His precious blood. The threat of failure, judgment, and condemnation has been removed. Knowing that God's love for us and approval of us will never be determined by our performance is the most encouraging promise to which we cling. Oh what a Savior! In Your mighty Name Above All Names—Friend, we pray, amen.

Look Up—meditate on John 15:13

Look In—as you meditate on John 15:13 pray to see how you might apply it to your life.

Look Out—as you meditate on John 15:13 pray to see how you might apply it to your relationships with others.

Notes

I am the good shepherd. The good shepherd lays down his life for the sheep.

Good Shepherd John 10:11

John 10:11

7 Good Shepherd

Good Shepherd from John 10:11 …

NASB: I am the good shepherd; the good shepherd lays down His life for the sheep.

Amplified: I am the Good Shepherd. The Good Shepherd risks and lays down His [own] life for the sheep.

J. B. Phillips: I am the good shepherd. The good shepherd will give his life for the sake of his sheep.

The Message: I am the Good Shepherd. The Good Shepherd puts the sheep before himself, sacrifices himself if necessary.

Psalm 23 is perhaps the most beloved scripture about our Good Shepherd. I wanted to share this wonderful verse-by-verse study of Psalm 23 by Dr. Warren W. Wiersbe from *The Transformation Study Bible*:

Psalm 23:1—The present tense verb "is" means, "the Lord is shepherding me," indicating an ongoing relationship. Eastern shepherds guarded their sheep, led them, provided food and water for them; took care of them when they were wearied, bruised, cut or sick; rescued them when they strayed; knew their names; assisted in delivering the lambs; and in every way simply loved them.

23:2—The word translated, "leads," in verse 2 means "to lead gently." You cannot drive sheep. The sheep hear the shepherd's voice and follow him, just as we listen to Christ in His Word and obey Him.

23:3—God cares for us because He loves us and wants us to glorify Him. The shepherd cares for his sheep because he loves them and wants to maintain his own good reputation as a faithful shepherd.

23:4a—This is the central verse of the psalm, and the personal pronoun changes from "he" to "you." David is not speaking about the shepherd, but speaking to the shepherd. In the dark valley, God is not before us but beside us, leading the way and calming our fears. The "darkest valley" represents any difficult experience of life that makes us afraid, and that includes death.

23:4b—Sheep lack good vision and are easily frightened in new circumstances, especially when it's dark. The presence of the shepherd calms them.

23:4c—The rod was a heavy cudgel with which the shepherd could stun or kill an attacking beast, and the staff was the shepherd's crook, which he used to assist the individual sheep.

23:5a—Another word for "feast" is "table." This table doesn't necessarily refer to a piece of furniture used by humans, for the word simply means, "something spread out." Flat places in the hilly country were called "tables," and sometimes the shepherd stopped the flock at these "tables" and allowed them to eat and rest as they headed for the fold.

23:5b—The shepherd would examine the sheep as they entered the fold to be sure none of them was bruised, injured, or sick from eating a poisonous plant. To the wounds, he applied the soothing oil, and for the thirsty, he had his large two-handled cup filled with water. He would also apply the oil to the heads and the horns of the sheep to help keep the flies and other insects away. The sheep knew they were safe, and they could sleep without fear.

23:6—As the shepherd lay each night at the door of the sheepfold, he looked back over the day and gave thanks that the Lord had blessed them with goodness and mercy. Dr. Harry Ironside used to say that goodness and mercy are the two sheepdogs that help keep the sheep where they belong. We live our lives one day at a time, because God built the universe to run one day at a time. There must be a time for labor and a time for rest. When we try to live two or three days at a time, we cannot enjoy today. Eventually, this catches up with us physically, emotionally and spiritually. As an old man, David looked back over his long life and came to the same conclusion. In spite of his sins and failures, he had been followed by goodness and mercy, which is the Old Testament equivalent of Romans 8:28. Under the old covenant, the sheep died for the shepherd, but under the new covenant, the Shepherd died for the sheep—and we shall meet our Shepherd in heaven! "For the Lamb on the throne will be their Shepherd. He will lead them to springs of life-giving water. And God will wipe every tear from their eyes" (Rev. 7:17). As David looked ahead, he knew he would be in heaven—the Father's house—forever.

When I am praying, I picture Jesus Christ, my Good Shepherd, in the green pasture of the 23rd Psalm. As I pray, I take whatever concern I have, or the person for whom I am interceding by the hand. I walk out to the meadow, the green pasture, and I place my concern, or the hand of the person for whom I am interceding, in Jesus' hand…knowing that He is sovereign, He loves me, and He loves the person for whom I am interceding more than I do. He has a plan, a hope, and a future for each of us…and I walk away, thanking God for how He is working in my life and in the lives of those for whom I am interceding. I experience a feeling of peace…as Catherine Marshall prayed, Lord, I trust You…You know what You're doing…I relinquish my will to Yours.

Good Shepherd, we ask you to wrap Your Loving Arms around us today. You are close to the brokenhearted and You save those who are crushed in spirit. You are our Good Shepherd, we lack nothing. You make us lie down in green pastures, You lead us beside the still waters. You restore our souls. You lead us in the path of righteousness for Your name's sake. Even when we walk through the valley of the shadow of death, we will fear no evil, for You are with us. You are Emmanuel, God with us, we are absolutely certain, You are with us at this time. Your rod and Your staff, Your Holy Spirit and Your Word, they comfort us. You prepare a table before us in the presence of our enemies. You anoint our heads with oil, our cup overflows with blessings. Surely goodness and mercy will follow us all the days of our lives and we will dwell in the house of the Lord forever. In Your mighty Name Above All Names—Good Shepherd, we pray, amen.

Look Up—meditate on John 10:11

Look In—as you meditate on John 10:11 pray to see how you might apply it to your life.

Look Out—as you meditate on John 10:11 pray to see how you might apply it to your relationships with others.

The Spirit of the Lord
is upon me;
because he has anointed me
to preach good news
to the poor.
He has sent me to bind up
the brokenhearted,
to proclaim liberty to the captives,
and an opening
of the eyes
to the blind.

Healer
ISAIAH 61:1

Isaiah 61:1

& Healer

Healer from Isaiah 61:1…

NASB: The Spirit of the Lord God is upon me, because the Lord has anointed me to bring good news to the afflicted; He has sent me to bind up the brokenhearted, to proclaim liberty to captives and freedom to prisoners.

Amplified: The Spirit of the Lord God is upon me, because the Lord has anointed and qualified me to preach the Gospel of good tidings to the meek, the poor, and afflicted; He has sent me to bind up and heal the brokenhearted, to proclaim liberty to the [physical and spiritual] captives and the opening of the prison and of the eyes to those who are bound,

Expanded: The Lord God has put his Spirit in me, because the Lord has ·appointed [anointed] me to ·tell [bring] the good news to the poor. He has sent me to ·comfort [bind up] those whose hearts are broken, to tell the captives they are free, and to tell the prisoners they are released.

God's Word: The Spirit of the Almighty Lord is with me because the Lord has anointed me to deliver good news to humble people. He has sent me to heal those who are brokenhearted, to announce that captives will be set free and prisoners will be released.

The Message: The Spirit of God, the Master, is on me because God anointed me. He sent me to preach good news to the poor, heal the heartbroken, Announce freedom to all captives, pardon all prisoners.

Pastor Harry Ironside writes: "In Isaiah Chapter 61, we have the portion to which the Lord Jesus directed His hearers' attention when He went into the synagogue at Nazareth. After His baptism in the Jordan and His temptation in the wilderness He came up through Judea—He gave the Word in Judea—into Galilee and entered into the city where He had been brought up--Nazareth. There, we are told, that as His custom was on a Sabbath day, He went into the synagogue. That is very significant. We have very little information as to the early days of the Lord Jesus Christ, and men have tried to imagine what may have taken place between His childhood and His thirtieth year, when He went forth to be baptized by John, as He consecrated Himself to His great work. People have tried to imagine what Jesus may have done during those years, but Scripture says that when some of His townspeople came to hear Him, they said: "Is not this the carpenter?" They had known Him as a carpenter. And Luke says that He went as His custom was on the Sabbath day into the synagogue. It shows that the Lord Jesus not only submitted Himself to the obedience of the laws divinely given, but also to the ordinary regulations of the rabbis, and attended the synagogue service and apparently took part in it. They would recognize Him as one who had a right to go up to the dais and read from the Holy Scriptures. In that synagogue at Nazareth was handed to Him the book of the prophet Isaiah; this book, the last part, too, of this book - and it is called the prophet Isaiah. "The Spirit of the Lord God is upon me; because the Lord hath anointed me to preach good tidings unto the meek; he hath sent me to bind up the brokenhearted, to proclaim liberty to the captives, and the opening of the prison to them that are bound; To proclaim the acceptable year of the Lord" (verses 1, 2a). Then He closed the book. He read to the middle of the sentence but then He closed the book. Why did He not go on with Isaiah's words? Because those verses tell what He came to do at His first coming. His first and His second comings are intimately linked together in this chapter of Isaiah. He came to preach deliverance to captives, He came to give sight to the blind, to open the prisons of those that are bound, He came to proclaim the acceptable year of the Lord. There He stopped at what we would call a comma. He put this whole dispensation in which you and I live into that comma. It is the acceptable year of the Lord still. We have not moved one iota beyond that point where He closed the book. Why did He close it there? Because the rest of the sentence would carry us on into the day of the Lord after this present age has come to an end. So now is the accepted time, now is the day of salvation. He came to proclaim the acceptable year of the Lord."

Often when we thank God, we are responding to what He does, how He is answering our prayers and working out His plan in our lives. When we worship, on the other hand, we are adoring, honoring, and embracing God simply for who He is. Worship is the overflow of hearts that are thankful and full of wonder. We worship Jesus when we lift our hearts and voices in grateful acknowledgment of how He has revealed Himself in our lives: our faithful and trustworthy provider, protector, redeemer, refuge, comforter, healer, sustainer, source of strength, helper, father, and friend. With praise-filled hearts we can proclaim all that God is and has done in our lives. Nothing delights the heart of our Father more than songs of praise from the lips of his children. It's what we were created for, and it deepens our dependence on Him. What an awesome God we serve! Express to the Lord your desire to worship Him with all your heart, soul, and mind. Spend time in His presence meditating on all God has done and who He is to you.

Lord Jesus, how I praise the wonders of Your works! May I be found faithful in proclaiming through a heart of praise all that you are and have done in my life. You are so many things to me—You are everything! Thank you for the privilege of receiving a heart that is able to praise you every single day of my life. You are my Healer. I ask You to reveal this in my life today. Thank You for revealing Your wondrous attributes to us in Your Word. As I read it, continually open my eyes to who You really are so that my prayers will rest on the solid foundation of Your character. May my prayers have power because they are based on the truth about You. In Your mighty Name Above All Names—Healer, we pray, amen.

Look Up—meditate on Isaiah 61:1

Look In—as you meditate on Isaiah 61:1 pray to see how you might apply it to your life.

Look Out—as you meditate on Isaiah 61:1 pray to see how you might apply it to your relationships with others.

Therefore the Lord himself will give you a sign. Behold, the virgin will conceive, and bear a son, and shall call His name Immanuel.

Immanuel — ISAIAH 7:14

Isaiah 7:14

9 Immanuel

Immanuel from Isaiah 7:14...

NASB: Therefore the Lord Himself will give you a sign: Behold, a virgin will be with child and bear a son, and she will call His name Immanuel.

Amplified: Therefore the Lord Himself shall give you a sign: Behold, the young woman who is unmarried and a virgin shall conceive and bear a son, and shall call his name Immanuel [God with us].

NET: For this reason the sovereign master himself will give you a confirming sign. Look, this young woman is about to conceive and will give birth to a son. You, young woman, will name him Immanuel.

NLT: All right then, the Lord himself will give you the sign. Look! The virgin will conceive a child! She will give birth to a son and will call him Immanuel (which means 'God is with us').

The Voice: Suit yourself. The Lord will give you a proof-sign anyway: See, a young maiden will conceive. She will give birth to a son and name Him Immanuel, that is, "God with us."

Young's Literal: Therefore the Lord Himself giveth to you a sign, Lo, the

Virgin is conceiving, And is bringing forth a son, And hath called his name Immanuel.

In March, 2000, I traveled to Israel with 850 other women for the filming of the Beth Moore Bible Study, Jesus, the One and Only. As our Israeli tour bus drove toward Bethlehem, I began to wonder, what would it have been like for Joseph and Mary as they approached Bethlehem 20 centuries ago? Was the five-mile stretch of road from Jerusalem as bustling as it is today? What did they see? What did they hear?

As we approach the town, we notice all the terraced olive groves, which march up the dry hills like steps leading to a temple. And then, suddenly, there it is: Bethlehem, the ancient "House of Bread"--clinging to a ridge as if clinging to history itself. O, little town of Bethlehem, how still we see thee lie!

Naturally, no one can be sure exactly where Jesus' birth occurred in Bethlehem, but you just know that, wherever the exact spot, it couldn't have been far away. That thought alone pierces through all the touristy glitz and fairly takes your breath away in anticipation.

Standing in the city of Bethlehem, looking out on the Shepherd's Fields I can just imagine the heavens opening up and the angels descending and shouting, Glory to God in the highest, unto to you is born this day in the city of David a Savior which is Christ the Lord. When the shepherds in the field were surprised by the appearances of the angel and the heavenly host, their initial terror quickly turned to joy. Just as the angel had said, they found the baby, wrapped in cloths and lying in a manger. For these simple men with open hearts, it was a process of surprise, shock, fear, disbelief, hope, trust, confirmation, and finally indescribable joy! Joy at seeing the Christ child. Joy at having been singled out for the unique honor of being present at the very moment in history when God came near. Joy at having witnessed the one birth that gives meaning to all other births.

Bible Teacher Beth Moore writes: "When Mary heard those first cries of divine life wrapped in human flesh, any thought of disappointment must surely have turned into immeasurable peace and joy! Even His name, Immanuel, "El" means "God," the rest of the word means "with us," the "with us God." He created us to be with us. He gave each of us a longing for Him by creating every single human being with a "with" need. While the world carried on unconcerned, the infant Immanuel cooed and kicked and toddled His way to His feet. God, the Immortal Invisible, walked among His people, Israel, as they sojourned through the wilderness. But not until now did His invisible feet sink into the sand, shod with skin, making visible prints. And God was with us. Immanuel."

What do we learn from the unlikely circumstances of Jesus' birth, but that our God is a God of surprises. How He delights in bringing us unexpected joy! How many times have we seen God most clearly in the middle of a crisis? How many times have we discovered the miraculous in the midst of the mundane?

Pastor Charles Swindoll writes: "Immanuel. God with us. He who resided in Heaven, co-equal and co-eternal with the Father and the Spirit, willingly descended into our world. He breathed our air, felt our pain, knew our sorrows, and died for our sins. He didn't come to frighten us, but to show us the way to warmth and safety."

Where is God when we're in the emergency room with a severely injured loved one? When trouble or tragedy strikes, we long for God, the living God. Uncomfortable circumstances may continue, but God will prove himself our sure refuge because he has promised he will never forsake us. His name, Immanuel, means "God with us." Because of this truth we can continue to call on the Lord with confidence that He will hear and respond because of His unfailing love.

Lord Jesus, our Immanuel, thank You that You are the "with us God." Thank You for Your promised presence with me today. Although my circumstances may seem overwhelming, I call to You with confidence because You are all powerful and You love me. I praise You that you are Immanuel—God with us—in everything we experience as we walk through this broken, hurting world. Help me to be Your hands and feet today, Your words of comfort and encouragement to those who need to know "where You are" in their times of deep need. In Your mighty Name Above All Names—Immanuel, we pray, amen.

Look Up—meditate on Isaiah 7:14

Look In—as you meditate on Isaiah 7:14 pray to see how you might apply it to your life.

Look Out—as you meditate on Isaiah 7:14 pray to see how you might apply it to your relationships with others.

Revelation 5:5

Lion of Judah — REV. 5:5

One of the elders said to me, "Don't weep. Behold, the Lion who is of the tribe of Judah, the Root of David, has overcome: He who opens the book and its seven seals."

10 Lion of Judah

Lion of Judah from Revelation 5:5 ...

NASB: and one of the elders said to me, "Stop weeping; behold, the Lion that is from the tribe of Judah, the Root of David, has overcome so as to open the book and its seven seals."

Amplified: Then one of the elders [of the heavenly Sanhedrin] said to me, Stop weeping! See, the Lion of the tribe of Judah, the Root (Source) of David, has won (has overcome and conquered)! He can open the scroll and break its seven seals!

CEV: Then one of the elders said to me, "Stop crying and look! The one who is called both the 'Lion from the Tribe of Judah' and 'King David's Great Descendant' has won the victory. He will open the book and its seven seals."

Expanded: But one of the elders said to me, "Do not cry! [Look; Behold] The Lion from the tribe of Judah [a messianic title; Gen. 49:9–10], David's descendant [the root of David; a messianic title applied to Christ; Is. 11:10], has won the victory [overcome; conquered] so that he is able to open the scroll and its seven seals."

J. B. Phillips: one of the elders said to me, "Do not weep. See, the Lion from the tribe of Judah, the root of David, has won the victory and is able to open the book and break its seven seals."

Pastor Ray Stedman writes: "The Lion of the tribe of Judah" and "the Root of David" are both Jewish titles. They refer to prophecies from the Old Testament that predict there would be one from the tribe of Judah and from the family of David who would at last rule over the earth and solve its problems. These titles refer, then, to the King of the Jews -- the very title which Pilate inscribed on the Cross of Jesus. The King of the Jews! He is the One who triumphs by his death and is able to bring about God's kingdom on the earth. But, when John turns to see the conquering Lion of Judah, what he sees is the slain Redeemer of the world! He expected to see a Lion but what he saw was a Lamb, with the marks of death still upon him. Those marks of death are still upon the Lamb, and will be for all eternity. In these two symbols, the Lion of Judah and the Lamb that was slain, John sees the uniting of two themes that run throughout the Bible, Old Testament and New Testament alike. Lions are a symbol of majesty, power, rule and authority. Lions conquer; lambs submit! Lions roar; lambs die! There is introduced to us here the One who conquers by submitting. The symbols tie together the earthly promises of Israel and the heavenly calling of the church. This uniting of the Lion and the Lamb is the basis for C. S. Lewis' novels called "The Narnia Chronicles." A great Lion, Aslan, rules in majesty and roars in triumph, but he does so because he submits to being put to death by the evil characters controlled by the White Witch, but at last the kingdom of Narnia is freed from its bondage to winter and the springtime of the world arrives. It is a beautiful use of these symbols. As the Lion of Judah, Jesus will rule the world with a rod of iron. As the Lion of Judah our Lord reigns, but if anyone is weak and faltering, helpless or hopeless, he or she will find a compassionate Savior—because this Lion is also a Lamb! As the Lamb of God he is filled with mercy and grace, but if any should presume upon that grace and begin to live a rebellious or defiant life, let him beware—because this Lamb is also a Lion!"

Author C. S. Lewis was a Christian, and followers of the faith widely believe he wrote the Chronicles of Narnia series as a Christian allegory. An unpublished letter written by the author of the books himself has provided decisive evidence of the Christian message deeply imbedded in the Narnia books. A letter sent by C. S. Lewis to a child fan in 1961 reveals that Lewis was referring to Jesus Christ as he portrayed the mystical land and its savior—the Lion Aslan. The letter tells the child: "The whole Narnian story is about Christ." The clear letter has been made public by Walter Hooper, who is a literary advisor to the Lewis estate. In his newly publicized letter, Lewis states, "Supposing there really was a world like Narnia…and supposing Christ wanted to go into that world and save it (as He did ours) what might have happened?" Lewis concluded, "The stories are my answer. Since Narnia is a world of talking beasts, I thought he would become a talking beast there as he became a man here. I pictured him becoming a Lion there because the Lion is supposed to be the king of beasts; Christ is called 'the Lion of Judah' in the Bible."

Pastor Walter Scott writes: "And I wept much because no one had been found worthy to open the book nor to regard it. And one of the elders says to me, Do not weep. Behold, the Lion which (is) of the tribe of Judah, the Root of David, has overcome (so as) to open the book and its seven seals." The grief of the Seer is emphasized by the use of the pronoun "I," which is emphatic in the Greek. "I wept much." John is here regarded as the representative of the prophetic feeling at "the time of the end," or "the last days." His soul is stirred within him as his eye rests on the sealed scroll lying on the open hand of the Sitter on the throne, with no one in the vast creation of God competent to disclose its contents and carry them into execution. The tears of John have been termed "the weakness of the creature," but if "wept much" is sometimes the expression of weakness, it is equally the expression of a right and godly feeling. It has been remarked, "Without tears the Revelation was not written, neither without tears can it be understood." But the book was to be opened. And since worship of the highest order and an intimate knowledge of the mind of God are characteristics of the crowned and glorified elders or representatives of the redeemed, it is one of these elders who consoles the weeping Seer by directing his attention to One in every respect qualified to unfold the divine counsels and carry them to a triumphant issue. Who is He? The Lion of the tribe of Judah, the Root of David. What has He done? He has overcome every spiritual power by His death on the cross. Thus He has an unchallenged right in Himself, and because, too, of what He has done, to advance to the right hand of the Eternal, take the book, and effectuate the counsels of God."

Sometimes it seems as if the forces of evil are winning and godless rulers and superpowers are dominating our world. This scripture about the Lion of Judah reminds us of who is really in charge and calling the shots: the Lord Almighty. The same God who created the world with a word can shatter the plans of the nations and thwart all their schemes. No matter how out of control things may appear, God's plan remains in place. He is running the show and knows the end from the beginning. No one is higher or mightier than our Lord Jesus Christ—the Lion of Judah! He governs our world, His kingdom will come, and His sovereign will shall be done on earth as it is in heaven! God's intentions can never be shaken, and his plans stand firm forever. His amazing power is at work in the world, and He will carry out his eternal purpose to the last detail.

Thank you, Lord Jesus, for the assurance Your Word gives me that You reign over heaven and earth and that no one can thwart your plans for my life—and for the whole world. I put my trust in You today. Only You understand everything—even those things that are mysteries to me. Because you have all authority on earth and in heaven, I can rest in You. You are my shield and my eternal protector. When I am in danger or distress, help me trust in You. Lift my gaze and my heart from everything on this earth to You, who reign over all. Thank you for answering me from heaven and acting on my behalf when I cry out to you. May You be glorified in my life. In Your mighty Name Above All Names—Lion of Judah, we pray, amen.

Look Up—meditate on Revelation 5:5

Look In—as you meditate on Revelation 5:5 pray to see how you might apply it to your life.

Look Out—as you meditate on Revelation 5:5 pray to see how you might apply it to your relationships with others.

Notes

King of Kings

Revelation 19:16

I saw the heaven opened, and behold, a white horse, and He who sat on it is called Faithful and True. He has on His garment and on His thigh a name written, "King of Kings and Lord of Lords."

Revelation 19:11, 16

11 King of Kings

King of Kings from Revelation 19:16...

NASB: And on His robe and on His thigh He has a name written, "KING OF KINGS, AND LORD OF LORDS."

Amplified: And on His robe and on His thigh He has a name inscribed, "KING OF KINGS, AND LORD OF LORDS."

J.B Phillips: Written upon his cloak and upon his thigh is the name, KING OF KINGS AND LORD OF LORDS.

The Message: On his robe and thigh is written, King of kings, Lord of lords.

Young's Literal: and he hath upon the garment and upon his thigh the name written, `King of kings, and Lord of lords.'

Pastor Thomas L. Constable writes: "The robe is a symbol of majesty, and the thigh suggests power. Evidently the name appeared on the part of Christ's robe that covered His thigh, which would be most conspicuous. The title "King of kings" is one that Persian and later rulers of empires ascribed to themselves but only the Messiah qualifies for it in its true sense. People living on earth at the time of the Second Coming will see Jesus Christ return. What a contrast this coming is with the Lord Jesus' first coming: as a baby, in humility and obscurity, riding a donkey into Jerusalem rather than a horse, coming to die rather than to reign."

Pastor Arno Gaebelein has written: "And He had a name written, that no man knew but Himself." And again it is written, "His Name is called the Word of God." And on His vesture and on His thigh there is a name written, "King of Kings and Lord of Lords." The unknown Name is the name of His essential deity. No human name can express what He is in Himself, "No man knoweth the Son but the Father." His Name "the Word of God" refers us to the Gospel of John. As the Word He is the express image of God, that is, He makes God visible. He is the expression of God in His character, His thoughts and counsels. And the third name mentioned, "King of Kings and Lord of Lords," expresses what He is in relation to the earth."

Pastor Tony Garland writes: "King of kings is *basileus basileōn*. Lord of lords is *kyrios kyriōn*. Each phrase involves two words which have the same lexeme in a relationship indicating the supreme member: the supreme King among kings, the supreme Lord among lords…All of these various heads and horns had contested for the position which alone belongs to Christ, the King of kings. Christ will obtain the kingdom, but it will be achieved according to the will of the Father."

Pastor J. Ramsey Michaels wrote: "Here many crowns on a single head suggest many spheres of sovereignty under a single Lord, anticipating the inscription KING OF KINGS AND LORD OF LORDS finally made explicit at the end of the account. This inscription is a traditional formula that is to be understood quite literally. The rider on the white horse is about to be seen precisely as a King victorious over all other kings, and as supreme Lord, victorious over "generals and mighty men" and their armies."

Pastor S. Lewis Johnson has said: "John concludes this section with another name in the sixteenth verse, "And on His robe and on His thigh He has a name written, 'King of Kings and Lord of Lords'." That's a word directed first of all to Domitian who liked to parade in the 1st Century in Rome as "God the Lord". He had himself proclaimed Emporator twenty-two times. When he rode in past the peoples, the poets cried out, "*Prīnceps prīncepum summa ducis*," the prince of the princes and the highest of the leaders. In other words, Domitian was an antecedent of Ceaușescu and Hitler and all of the rest of these communist puppets who like to have themselves exalted constantly before the people with their pictures everywhere and everybody bowing to them as sovereigns of their little empires."

Much of the book of Revelation is puzzling and beyond our understanding; it pictures something that we will experience only in the hereafter. Now we comprehend only snippets of the great panorama of the end of time. As the heavenly company gathers, the twenty-four elders fall down before God, lay their crowns before him, and unite in praise: "You are worthy! You created everything." Just as the twenty-four elders lay down their crowns, we are to lay down our best efforts, our victories, and ministries, and bow in worship. We have nothing that we haven't received from God. Corrie ten Boom said that after she spoke, people often showered her with accolades and compliments. But when she got back to her room, she would bow before the Lord and—just like a bouquet—offer to him every word of praise she had received. Someday every knee will bow, and we will join the elders and the company of heaven to worship the King of kings, but in the meantime, we can still worship the creator and sustainer of the universe, who is worthy to receive all glory and honor and power.

Lord Jesus, our mighty King of kings, thank You for the pictures in Revelation of your glory being celebrated in heaven. You are worthy! It is for You and because of You that all things exist. Give us glimpses of how infinite, limitless, and majestic You are so that Your glory is our focus. Draw us into worship. I lay my crowns before You, Lord—all that I've done or accomplished, all that I am, I give to You. In Your mighty Name Above All Names—King of kings, we pray, amen.

Look Up—meditate on Revelation 19:16

Look In—as you meditate on Revelation 19:16 pray to see how you might apply it to your life.

Look Out—as you meditate on Revelation 19:16 pray to see how you might apply it to your relationships with others.

*I am the light of the world.
He who follows me
will not walk in darkness,
but will have
the light of life.*

Light of the World

JOHN 8:12

John 8:12

12 Light of the World

Light of the World from John 8:12 ...

NASB: Then Jesus again spoke to them, saying, "I am the Light of the world; he who follows Me will not walk in the darkness, but will have the Light of life."

Amplified: Once more Jesus addressed the crowd. He said, I am the Light of the world. He who follows Me will not be walking in the dark, but will have the Light which is Life.

Expanded: Later, Jesus talked to the people again, saying, "I am the light of the world [the Feast of Shelters included a lamp lighting ritual that Jesus may be alluding to; 7:37–39]. The person who follows me will never ·live [walk] in darkness but will have the light ·that gives life [of life]."

J. B. Phillips: Later, Jesus spoke to the people again and said, "I am the light of the world. The man who follows me will never walk in the dark but will live his life in the light."

Living Bible: Later, in one of his talks, Jesus said to the people, "I am the

Light of the world. So if you follow me, you won't be stumbling through the darkness, for living light will flood your path."

The Message: Jesus once again addressed them: "I am the world's Light. No one who follows me stumbles around in the darkness. I provide plenty of light to live in."

Pastor John MacArthur writes: "In John's gospel, Jesus makes a claim, He says He's God, He claims to be Messiah and men react ninety-nine percent of the time violently. In this passage we see the very same thing, only it's a fresh new beautiful look at Jesus Christ. In this one Christ makes the same claims using a different metaphor and then we see the reaction again and how Christ meets that. So we come again to a direct confrontation between the claims of Christ and the reaction of men who heard those claims. This particular claim of Jesus is no different than His others, but He couches it in the phrase, "I am the light of the world." There's no question about the fact that we live in a dark world. I'm talking about the darkness that settles on the soul of men, I'm talking about a moral darkness. Man is by his own appetites and his own passions pushing himself further and further into that darkness for man's passions and appetites tell him to seek the good life where the good life isn't found. Jesus said there is light. He said I am that light. We have proclaimed that light, it's in the Word of God. God's written it in the hearts of men, there's light. Jesus is that light. And that's the message of this passage, that Jesus is the light of the world. For those who are willing to come to Him, He's there, but it's going to demand that you be exposed. You see, before you can ever come to Jesus Christ to find the light, to receive Jesus Christ as Savior, the light's going to turn on bright and show you what you are. That's why repentance comes before salvation, at the very beginning. First we repent and then God redeems us supernaturally. You've got to be aware of what you are. Jesus is the light. Why is He called light? To the darkness of falsehood He is the light of truth. To the darkness of ignorance He is the light of wisdom. To the darkness of impurity He is the light of holiness. To the darkness of sorrow He is the light of joy. To the darkness of death He's the light of life. He is called light because the world is dark and the antithesis of darkness is light. He is everything the world isn't. Jesus is saying nothing more and nothing less at this point than I am your Messiah. He was not only claiming to be Messiah, He was claiming to be God. The psalmist said this, "The Lord is my light." And when Jesus said I am the light He was saying I'm God. That's quite a claim. When Jesus came along and said, "I am light," He was claiming, number one, to be Messiah, number two, to be God. Same claim, just different metaphor. He used so many different ways to say the same thing."

Pastor John MacArthur continues: "Why does Jesus particularly choose this metaphor? When He said "I am the light of the world" He said the most devastating dramatic thing, it's just unbelievable. Now the feast of tabernacles had just concluded. It was seven days long. It was a yearly thing and it was to commemorate the wandering of Israel in the wilderness. Remember the 40 years they wandered? This was a commemoration feast of that to keep them to remember that God had blessed them during those 40 years. In the evening this ritual took place and the illumination of the temple ritual was to commemorate, mark it, the light in the wilderness that had led Israel. Now you remember that during the day they were led by a light that looked like a cloud. And at night they were led by a pillar of fire, flaming light in the sky. They had been led by light in the daytime, the light as like a cloud moving through the sky. They were led at night by a flaming light, the pillar of fire. To commemorate the light that led them, they had this ceremony called the illumination of the temple which commemorated the light that led Israel in the Old Testament. They had this ceremony in the Court of the Women, that's why Jesus is there. That's why He went there to say, "I'm the light of the world." In the middle of the Court of the Women they erected giant candelabras, gigantic massive things with a multiplicity of lights that reflected up. And at night, in the evening, they would light all those candelabras and that light would just stream out of the top of that courtyard and flood the city of Jerusalem. In fact, the rabbis used to say that every courtyard in Jerusalem was lit all night, like a brilliant diamond flashing its light over the entire city of Jerusalem, the light just came pouring out of the top of that temple courtyard in the Court of the Women they did it. And they actually had places where people could sit around it. At the same time it was the noisiest celebration of the feast because everybody sang and they sang certain Psalms and they had certain dancing that they did and all this noise went on all night long while this light kept burning. And that light was to commemorate the light in the wilderness. Now that you have it in your mind, has it become reasonable to see what Jesus was doing? He walks into the Court of the Women and the light is long out cause the feast ended the day before, but sitting in the middle of that place is this gigantic candelabra. Jesus steps into the middle of this courtyard where there's nothing on their minds perhaps any more significant than seeing this candelabra and remembering the great illumination of Jerusalem. And they walk in there and they see that candelabra and Jesus steps up beside that candelabra and undoubtedly with some gesture says, "I am the light of the world." What a dramatic statement. For in their minds they would be remembering a light in Jerusalem that commemorated a light that led Israel. But Jesus says, "Yes, you remember the light last night in the temple here which made you remember the light that led Israel...I am the light of the world." Now do you see the significance of that statement? Talk about dramatics, Jesus was the master. He took that scene and made it so dynamic and so dramatic, He must have stunned them. You saw a light that lit Jerusalem, you celebrate a light that lit the wilderness, I am the light of the world. What a statement."

Pastor John MacArthur concludes: "Then He says an interesting thing, He says, "He that follows Me shall not walk in darkness but shall of the light of life." Some lights don't go anywhere. They just hang there, most lights. You don't say...follow the light. Well, how do you follow the light, it's just there? There was one light that moved, it wasn't the light in the temple that commemorated it but it was the light in Israel, wasn't it, in the wilderness. Did it move? It moved every night and it moved every day, didn't it? And what did they do? They followed it, didn't they? Jesus says you're remembering that light that moved Israel around, follow Me...follow Me, I'm a light that's moving, too. You know, when you follow Jesus Christ you don't sit around. "I'm following You, Lord." This light moves. You better be ready to move. And you better be ready to go where that light takes you. And if you follow Him you'll never walk in darkness...never walk in darkness, just follow the light. What does it mean to follow Him? When we say to follow something what are we talking about? What does it mean to follow Christ? The word "follow" here in verse 12 is interesting, it has many meanings but it basically translates to follow. It's not burdensome to follow to Christ, is it? I mean, it's just like through green pastures, you know, beside still waters. That's how my Shepherd leads me. That's not burdensome. I tell you, once you get to following Jesus Christ, you don't look for any other leaders, do you? I don't want another shepherd."

Think of our Savior: Jesus is the Light of the World, our Counselor, our Good Shepherd. Prayerfully studying and meditating on the character traits and names of God is one of the most faith-building, encouraging things you can do for your spiritual life. It will dispel your anxiety and boost your faith. It will enable you to trust God more. Knowing the true character of God will renew and transform your mind with the truth, dissolve doubt, and breathe life into your soul. Saying aloud the attributes of the Lord and thinking about how you've experienced different aspects of His character can be a powerful act of worship. Ask God to reveal Himself to you in greater clarity than you've ever experienced before. The Light of the world draws you to our heavenly Father. It reveals your need for something and Someone greater than yourself, just as it did when the light blinded Paul physically but opened his spiritual eyes to the truth. It is that light that illuminates God's Word and gives you wisdom that comes from above. It is the light that calls you by name and tells you that you are precious to the Savior. No one can withstand the unbridled light of God, but in heaven we will bask in it. Praise God for the light that guides us, but worship Him as the Light of the world.

Heavenly Father, we thank You for Your truth, Your Word, for what we've learned. God, I thank You for Jesus Christ, the Light of the world. May He become more real, more precious to us each moment. God, we pray that the Light of Christ might shed upon some heart today. Lord Jesus, thank You for being a light to reveal God to the nations so that more people can know and worship our Father. Thank you for bringing us out of darkness and into your marvelous light. I want to shine your light everywhere I go so that everyone around me will be drawn to you. In Your mighty Name Above All Names—Light of the world, we pray, amen.

Look Up—meditate on John 8:12

Look In—as you meditate on John 8:12 pray to see how you might apply it to your life.

Look Out—as you meditate on John 8:12 pray to see how you might apply it to your relationships with others.

Revelation 22:16

I, Jesus, have sent my angel to testify these things to you for the assemblies.

Bright Morning Star
REV. 22:16

I am the root and the offspring of David, the Bright and Morning Star.

13 Bright Morning Star

Bright Morning Star from Revelation 22:16…

NASB: "I, Jesus, have sent My angel to testify to you these things [a]for the churches. I am the root and the descendant of David, the bright morning star."

Amplified: I, Jesus, have sent My messenger (angel) to you to witness and to give you assurance of these things for the churches (assemblies). I am the Root (the Source) and the Offspring of David, the radiant and brilliant Morning Star.

Expanded: "I, Jesus, have sent my angel to ·tell you [testify/witness to] these things for the churches. I am the ·descendant from the family of David [root and descendant/offspring of David; a messianic title applied to Jesus; 5:4; Is. 11:10], and I am the bright morning star [2:28; Num. 24:17; a messianic title]."

NLT: "I, Jesus, have sent my angel to give you this message for the churches. I am both the source of David and the heir to his throne.[a] I am the bright morning star."

Young's Literal: I, Jesus did send my messenger to testify to you these things concerning the assemblies; I am the root and the offspring of David, the bright and morning star!

Pastor Francis Frangipane writes about Christ, who Himself is the "bright Morning Star" (Revelation 22:16): "A day is coming before the rapture, before the second coming of Jesus Christ, when those who follow Christ will be positioned, like the morning star—in the right place at the right time—and they will herald Christ's return. They will come from every nation, people, tribe and tongue, yet they will be one, for Christ will have given them His glory (John 17:22)."

The word, dawns, comes from the Greek word *diaugazo* from *diá* which means through and *augázo* which means shine—literally "to shine through." This word was used to describe daylight breaking through the darkness of night, picturing the first gleams of the sun piercing the darkness.

Pastor Marvin Vincent writes, "The verb *diaugazo* is compounded of *dia* which means through, and *auge* which means sunlight, thus carrying the picture of light breaking through the gloom. In other words, the truths in the Bible will continue to point to the source of all truth, Christ, until He returns in glory."

The words, "morning star," come from the Greek word, *phosphoros* from *phos* which means light and *phero* which means to bring; in English the word phosphorus means a substance that glows in the dark—literally light bringing, light bearer or bringer or bringing morning light. The morning star was the name that Greeks assigned to the planet Venus which was the brightest object in the sky apart from the sun and moon and appeared sometimes as the evening star and sometimes as the morning star. In the desert, the morning star is so brilliant that it appears as though the sun were about to rise.

Theologian W. E. Vine writes that *phosphoros* is used of the morning star, as the light–bringer in 2 Peter 1:19, where it indicates the arising of the light of Christ as the personal fulfillment, in the hearts of believers, of the prophetic Scriptures concerning His coming to receive them to Himself. In the context, these images (day dawning and morning star arising) point to the *parousia* or the appearing of Jesus Christ. This was partially fulfilled at Messiah's first coming but will be fulfilled at His return, His light driving away the spiritual darkness of this present evil age. "I, Jesus, have sent My angel to testify to you these things for the churches. I am the root and the offspring of David, the bright morning star." Here, in Revelation 22:16, Christ triumphantly proclaims that He is the true "Morning Star."

The word, arises, comes from the Greek word, *anatello* from *aná,* which means up and *téllo,* which means, set out for a goal—literally, to cause to arise, spring up, or be up. It was used especially of things in natural creation, like the rising of the sun or moon.

The word, hearts, comes from the Greek word, *kardia,* is not used to refer literally to the physical heart, but describes the seat of the desires, feelings, affections, passions, and impulses. *Kardia* refers to the causative source of a person's psychological life in its various aspects, and with special emphasis upon thoughts—'heart, inner self, mind.' "Heart" refers to the volition (your will), the mind, and the desires.

Pastor John MacArthur comments on *kardia* noting that..."Throughout Scripture, as well as in many languages and cultures throughout the world, the heart is used metaphorically to represent the inner person, the seat of motives and attitudes, the center of personality. But in Scripture it represents much more than emotion, feelings. It also includes the thinking process and particularly the will. In Proverbs we are told, "As [a man] thinketh in his heart, so is he" (Proverbs 23:7, KJV). Jesus asked a group of scribes, "Why are you thinking evil in your hearts?" (Matthew 9:4)... The heart is the control center of mind and will as well as emotion. The problem that caused God to destroy the earth in the Flood was a heart problem. "Then the Lord saw that the wickedness of man was great on the earth, and that every intent of the thoughts of his heart was only evil continually" (Genesis 6:5). God has always been concerned above all else with the inside of man, with the condition of his heart. The second coming of Christ will have not only an externally transforming impact on the universe, but also an internally transforming impact (in your hearts) on those believers who are alive when Jesus returns, forever removing any of their remaining doubts. The perfect revelation of the Scriptures will be replaced with the perfect and complete revelation of Jesus Christ at the second coming."

Pastor Theodore Hiebert writes: "The truth that Christ is coming again must first arise in their hearts, like the morning star, giving assurance of coming day. Assured of His anticipated return, they will be alert to detect the gleams of dawn breaking through the darkness. Those who disregard the light of prophecy will not understand the significance of these harbingers of coming day. Such a living hope must have a transforming impact upon our daily lives."

What if today you don't feel like singing songs of joy? What if painful or difficult circumstances have stolen your joy? Frustrations assail you; burdens or responsibilities weigh your heart down, so that the last thing you want to do is sing with joy. Ask God for the grace to praise him; ask him to open your spiritual eyes so that you stand in awe of Him.

Lord Jesus Christ, our Bright Morning Star, we praise You for Who You are. Your glory is higher than the heavens. Your majesty fills the earth. We worship and adore you. Open our eyes to see Your unfailing love and goodness. Renew our trust in Your Word. With a word You brought into existence the stars in the heavens and held the seas in place. Nothing can thwart Your plans. Fill our hearts with songs of joy. You are worthy of our unending praise! You created the stars and turn darkness into dawn and day into night, I bow before You. Nothing can withstand your power! Thank you for your Word, which reminds me of Who You are and calls me back to devotion and truth. Keep me from evil, and guide me along the path of life. Thank you for the free gift of salvation, that we are justified on the basis of the finished work of Jesus Christ on the Cross. Thank You that, right now, we are under the completely sufficient imputed righteousness of Christ. Because we have placed our trust in the finished work of Jesus Christ, we are redeemed by His precious blood. The threat of failure, judgment, and condemnation has been removed. Knowing that God's love for us and approval of us will never be determined by our performance is the most encouraging promise to which we cling. Oh what a Savior! Jesus, we love You, it is in Your mighty Name Above All Names—Bright Morning Star, we pray, amen.

Look Up—meditate on Revelation 22:16

Look In—as you meditate on Revelation 22:16 pray to see how you might apply it to your life.

Look Out—as you meditate on Revelation 22:16 pray to see how you might apply it to your relationships with others.

Notes

Philippians 2:9-11

Name Above all Names

Therefore God also highly exalted Him,
and gave to Him the name
which is above every name,
that at the name of Jesus
every knee should bow...
and that every tongue should confess
that Jesus Christ is Lord,
to the glory of God the Father.

14 Name Above All Names

Name Above All Names from Philippians 2:9…

NIV: Therefore God exalted him to the highest place and gave him the name that is above every name.

AMP: For this reason also [because He obeyed and so completely humbled Himself], God has highly exalted Him and bestowed on Him the name which is above every name,

Expanded: So God raised [exalted] him to the highest place. God made his name [or gave him the name] greater than [far above] every other name

Lightfoot: But as was his humility, so also was his exaltation. God raised him to a preeminent height, and gave him a title and a dignity far above all dignities and titles else.

NLT: Therefore, God elevated him to the place of highest honor and gave him the name above all other names,

Phillips: That is why God has now lifted him so high, and has given him the name beyond all names.

Wuest: Because of which voluntary act of supreme self-renunciation, God also super-eminently exalted Him to the highest rank and power, and graciously bestowed upon Him THE NAME, the one which is above every name

The Apostle Paul is not referring here to the physical name as we think of it today but is using "name" as it was used in Scripture to represent the total person. In this sense, the Bible uses one's "name" to speak of the total person, as well as of the office, the rank, and the dignity attached to the person because of his position. Today we use a name as little more than a distinguishing mark or label to differentiate one person from other people. But in the world of the New Testament, the name concisely sums up all that a person is. One's whole character was somehow implied in the name. In this passage "name" speaks not only of the total Person of Christ but also speaks to His title which supersedes forever every title every given to anyone. In short, the Name of the Lord is what He is, it is Himself. Paul is presenting the divine paradox, foolish to the natural man—that the way up is down. That a cross precedes a crown. That the road of exaltation by the Father is paved by humble service to others for the Father's glory.

Pastor A. T. Robertson discussing the phrase "God highly exalted Him" writes that..."Because of Christ's voluntary humiliation God lifted Him above or beyond *huper* the state of glory which He enjoyed before the Incarnation. What glory did Christ have after the Ascension that He did not have before in heaven? What did He take back to heaven that He did not bring? Clearly, His humanity. He returned to heaven the Son of Man as well as the Son of God. It means that Jesus Christ still bears the scars of His crucifixion in His hands, side and feet, scars which will eternally testify to the New Covenant which He cut with all those who have placed their faith in Him. His covenant scars bear evidence that once genuinely saved, always saved, for once a sinner has entered covenant with Jesus, He will never break that covenant. This picture of the exalted God-Man retaining the scars of Calvary should comfort all believers regarding the absolute eternal security of their salvation."

Greek Scholar Kenneth Wuest writes: "That which was graciously bestowed was not "a name," but "the Name." The definite article ("to" = the) appears in the Greek text and refers to a particular name. The title, The Name, is a very common Hebrew title, denoting office, rank, dignity. The expression, "The Name of God" in the Old Testament, denotes the divine Presence, the divine Majesty, especially as the object of adoration and praise. The context here dwells upon the honor and worship bestowed on Him upon whom this name was conferred. The conferring of this title "The Name," was upon the Lord Jesus as the Son of Man. A Man, the Man Christ Jesus, who as Very God had voluntarily laid aside His expression of the glory of Deity during His incarnation, now has placed upon His shoulders all the majesty, dignity, and glory of Deity itself. It is the God-Man Who stooped to the depths of humiliation, Who is raised, not as God now, although He was all that, but as Man, to the infinite height of exaltation possessed only by Deity. It is the answer of our Lord's prayer, "And now, O Father, glorify thou me with thine own self with the glory which I had with thee before the world was." It is the glory of Deity, not now seen shining in infinite splendor as in His pre-incarnate state, but that glory shining in perfect contrast to and with His glorified humanity raised now to a place of equal dignity with Deity. It is the ideal and beautiful combination of the exaltation of Deity and the humility of Deity seen in incarnate Deity. The word given is the translation of the Greek word used when God in grace freely gives salvation to the believing sinner. It is so used in Romans 8:32 ("He who did not spare His own Son, but delivered Him up for us all, how will He not also with Him freely give *charizomai* us all things?" It was an act of grace on the part of God the Father toward the incarnate Son who had voluntarily assumed a subordinate position so as to function as the Sin-bearer on the Cross."

Author C. S. Lewis in *Mere Christianity* wrote: "I am trying here to prevent anyone from saying the really foolish thing that people often say about Him [Jesus Christ]: "I'm ready to accept Jesus as a great moral teacher, but I don't accept his claim to be God." That is the one thing we must not say. A man who was merely a man and said the sort of things Jesus said would not be a great moral teacher. He would either be a lunatic—on a level with a man who says he is a poached egg—or else he would be the Devil of Hell. You must make your choice. Either this man was, and is, the Son of God, or else a madman or something worse ...You can shut him up for fool, you can spit at him and kill him as a demon; or you can fall at his feet and call him Lord and God. But let us not come up with any patronizing nonsense about his being a great human teacher. He has not left that option open to us. He did not intend to."

Pastor Wayne Detzler writes: "The word "name" is a translation of the Greek word *onoma*. This word is most commonly identified by its root nom, which is seen in the Latin word *nomen* and the English and German word "name." It is also reflected in such a combination word as "pseudonym" (a false name) or "homonym" (a word or name which sounds the same), or "synonym" (a word which means the same). Thus the name of the true God became identified with the power of that deity. In the Septuagint Greek Old Testament the word onoma appears no fewer than 1,000 times. In Hebrew thinking, a name is identified with character, and the name of God is the repository of God's power. In the times of the patriarchs human names were still full of meaning. But by the dawn of New Testament times, names were much less indicative of character. In the New Testament the word onoma and its verb form, *onomazo* (to name someone), appear 228 times. The most significant use of "name" is in relation to God or Jesus. In fact, when Jesus declared that discipleship was to be His disciples' main ministry, He commanded them to baptize in the name (singular) of the Father, the Son, and the Holy Spirit (Matt. 28:19). This is the clearest New Testament reference to the Trinity."

Theologian Charles F. Moule wrote: "God, in the incarnation, bestowed upon the one who is on an equality with him an earthly name which has come to be, in fact, the highest of names, because service and self-giving are themselves the highest of divine attributes. Because of the incarnation, the human name, "Jesus," is acclaimed as the highest name; and the Man Jesus thus comes to be acclaimed as Lord, to the glory of God the Father. For Christians, the name above all other names is Jesus. The angelic messenger announced, "You shall call His name Jesus, for He will save His people from their sins." Jesus' name has become the most exalted and meaningful name on earth and in heaven. What's in that name? All the grace of God, all the wonder of redemption, all that we believe, and all that we are hoping for. We anticipate the indescribable glory of that day when every knee will bow and every tongue, by glad choice or by divine constraint, will praise that highest and holiest of all names--Jesus!"

Our natural human tendency is toward selfishness instead of sacrifice and service, but in a world that rewards self-promotion and puts celebrities on pedestals, God calls us to assume a lowly place—as Jesus did when he came to earth to serve, not to be served. This King of kings and Lord of all lords made Himself nothing and didn't cling to His rights as God but obediently humbled himself even to the point of dying on the cross. He is calling us to join his family of servants, to bend over the fallen and lift their load, to be His hands and feet, and to call others to come to His side.

Lord Jesus, thank You for giving me a heart which desires to please You rather than to impress people. Thank You for forgiving me for my selfishness and for focusing on my life, my needs, my problems. Thank You for helping me to care more about others and their needs and to have a servant's heart so that You can do Your work through me. In Your mighty Name Above All Names we pray, amen.

Look Up—meditate on Philippians 2:9

Look In—as you meditate on Philippians 2:9 pray to see how you might apply it to your life.

Look Out—as you meditate on Philippians 2:9 pray to see how you might apply it to your relationships with others.

Notes

I and the Father are one.

One God
JOHN 10:30

John 10:30

15 One God

One God from John 10:30…

    NASB: I and the Father are one.

    Amplified: I and the Father are One [in essence and nature].

    The Message: I and the Father are one heart and mind.

Pastor John Calvin writes: "He intended to meet the jeers of the wicked; for they might allege that the power of God did not at all belong to him, so that he could promise to his disciples that it would assuredly protect them. He therefore testifies that his affairs are so closely united to those of the Father, that the Father's assistance will never be withheld from himself and his sheep. For Christ does not argue about the unity of substance, but about the agreement which he has with the Father, so that whatever is done by Christ will be confirmed by the power of his Father."

Pastor Steven J. Cole wrote: "Jesus states, "I and the Father are one." "One" is neuter in Greek, not masculine, indicating that Jesus and His Father are not one person, but are one in essence. John 1:1 showed us that Jesus is fully God and yet distinct from the Father: "In the beginning was the Word, and the

Word was with God, and the Word was God." Jesus could not be "with God" if He were the same person as the Father, and yet He "was God." John consistently shows this throughout his Gospel. Jesus repeatedly claims to have been sent to earth by the Father, which indicates a distinction of persons. Also, He prays to the Father, which would be pointless if He and the Father were the same person. Yet Jesus is God. God exists eternally as one God in three distinct persons, each of whom is fully God. Jesus' statement that He and the Father are one does not mean that they are one person. So both here and consistently throughout the Gospel of John, Jesus' words show that He is God."

Pastor John MacArthur writes: "I and My Father are one." He means, "We're one in power, we're one in essence, we're one in work. Everything I do the Father does, we're one." He's talking about His indivisible union with God. Jesus is saying, "I'm God."

God's Word reveals what is necessary for effective prayer—the key is forgiveness. Although it is contrary to the world's pattern, it is at the heart of the life Jesus calls us to. Christ explained that holding grudges proves detrimental to our oneness with the Father. Our fellowship with God is restored through our own repentance and confession. Jesus provided for this through his finished work on the cross. He died so that we would be pardoned and restored to the Father. When we come to Jesus, he forgives our sins of the past and all the sins we will ever commit. But we who are forgiven much must love and forgive others much! Do you need to forgive someone today? What relationship needs restoration? Ask the Holy Spirit to show you any areas where you need to practice forgiveness. God is ready to provide the grace to enable us to forgive and to experience being fully forgiven ourselves.

Heavenly Father, thank You for giving me a forgiving heart, receiving Your forgiveness and forgiving those who have wronged me. Thank You for creating in me a free and forgiving spirit that sees others as You do, responds to them with Your heart, and prays for them with Your love. In mighty Name Above All Names—One God—Father, Son, and Holy Spirit, we pray, amen.

Look Up—meditate on John 10:30

Look In—as you meditate on John 10:30 pray to see how you might apply it to your life.

Look Out—as you meditate on John 10:30 pray to see how you might apply it to your relationships with others.

Notes

His name will be called
Wonderful, Counselor
Mighty God,
Everlasting Father,
Prince of Peace.

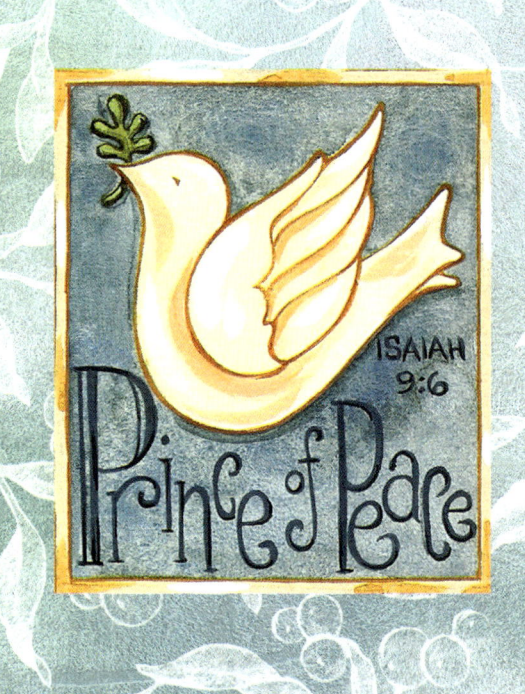

Prince of Peace
ISAIAH 9:6

Isaiah 9:6

16 Prince of Peace

Prince of Peace from Isaiah 9:6 ...

NASB: For a child will be born to us, a son will be given to us; And the government will rest on His shoulders; and His name will be called Wonderful Counselor, Mighty God, Eternal Father, Prince of Peace

Amplified: For to us a Child is born, to us a Son is given; and the government shall be upon His shoulder, and His name shall be called Wonderful Counselor, Mighty God, Everlasting Father [of Eternity], Prince of Peace.

Expanded Bible: A child ·has been [or will be; the prophet views the future as though it had already happened] born to us;·God has given a son [L a son has been given] to us. He will be responsible for leading the people [L The government/rule/dominion will be on his shoulder]. His name will be Wonderful Counselor [or Wonderful! Counselor!; or Extraordinary Advisor], Powerful [Mighty] God, Father Who Lives Forever [Eternal Father], Prince of Peace.

NET: For a child has been born to us, a son has been given to us. He shoulders responsibility and is called: Extraordinary Strategist, Mighty God, Everlasting Father, Prince of Peace

Pastor Ray Stedman writes: "The Greek word *eirene* is derived from the verb *"eiro"* which means to "join together." The picture is that of binding or joining together what is broken or divided—setting the divided parts at one again. To "make peace" is to join together that which is separated. Eirene originally meant the ordered life that was possible when people were not at war. Later, the concept was expanded to include an inner, personal peace. As noted above, in secular Greek eirene was originally associated with cessation or absence of war. Before we were born from above, we were "at war" with God. In Christ our lives are made whole, our relationships are harmonized, and we experience the spiritual and psychological wholeness that God intended for human beings in the original creation. His peace can provide freedom from disquieting or oppressive thoughts or emotions. Jesus did not end all human wars, but he does make it possible to end the war between God and man. His death is our peace, our means of reconciliation with our Father. Peace does not mean the absence of pain. It means that in our pain, we can have peace because we know the Prince of Peace and we know He is in control. True peace comes not the absence of conflict but from the presence of the Prince of Peace."

Jim Walton was translating the New Testament for the Muinane people of La Sabana in the jungles of Colombia. But he was having trouble with the word peace. During this time, Fernando, the village chief, was promised a 20-minute plane ride to a location that would have taken him 3 days to travel by walking. The plane was delayed in arriving at La Sabana, so Fernando departed on foot. When the plane finally came, a runner took off to bring Fernando back. But by the time he had returned, the plane had left. Fernando was livid because of the mix-up. He went to Jim and launched into an angry tirade. Fortunately, Walton had taped the chief's diatribe. When he later translated it, he discovered that the chief kept repeating the phrase, "I don't have one heart." Jim asked other villagers what having "one heart" meant, and he found that it was like saying, "There is nothing between you and the other person." That, Walton realized, was just what he needed to translate the word peace. To have peace with God means that there is nothing—no sin, no guilt, no condemnation—that separates us. And that peace with God is possible only through Christ.

Pastor Don Fortner writes: "In all that Christ has done as our Mediator, whether in planning or in executing the work of redemption, he has sought and secured the peace and eternal welfare of God's elect. It was to purchase our peace that he became incarnate and died upon the cross. It was to bestow peace upon us that he ascended into heaven, assumed the reins of universal dominion, and undertook the management of providence. Peace was the legacy which he left to his church when he departed from this world. Upon his ascension back into heaven, he poured out the Spirit of peace upon his people. To this very hour the Son of God, our Savior, the Prince of Peace dispenses peace according to his own sovereign will to the sons of men, giving it in great abundance to all the subjects of his kingdom. The word "prince" simply implies that Christ, at the time of his incarnation and birth, was the rightful, legal heir of the throne upon which he now sits. Christ is here called "The Prince." He is called the

Prince of Peace because it is his sovereign prerogative to speak peace to his people. And there is no peace in the world but that which he bestows. Christ alone is the Prince of Peace, and those who trust him enjoy "a peace which passes all understanding.". No one will ever apply to Christ for peace until they are in trouble and distress of soul, made to feel the danger, bitterness, and consequences of sin, and made to see the impossibility of helping themselves. But when weary, heavy laden sinners seek him, he hears their prayers and gives them peace. He steps out upon the bow of the troubled, tempest tossed ship, reveals himself in boundless, almighty grace, and says to their raging souls, "Peace be still"…and immediately there is a great calm."

Pastor Wayne Barber writes: "Now we need to understand that "Prince" means not only giver, but the one who maintains it. He gives the peace, and He maintains the peace. The first place that we find that peace needed is not with Jew and Gentile. It is with man and God. That peace was disrupted when Adam sinned. Man was separated from God, and was placed at enmity with God. You see the first thing that must be received is God's grace. God's grace is what God does to a man, in a man, for a man and through a man that a man can't do himself. God came down. Man could not ascend. He tried that in Genesis 11. That's where the nations came from. God came down as He told Nicodemus in John 3. He came down to die for our sin. The greatest picture of grace in all of Scripture is Jesus coming to die for our sin and shedding His blood to redeem us off the slave block of bondage to sin. When man receives God's grace, then and only then can he be at peace with the God that he has been estranged from since Adam's sin. So before you ever talk about peace with man, you've got to realize Jesus is the essence of our peace with God. So often we do it the reverse. So often there is a problem between two of us, and we try to major on our relationship to make our relationship with God better. No, you major on your relationship with God, and that makes your relationship with others what it ought to be. Jesus is the essence of God's peace, the essence of our peace with God."

What situation or problem could steal your sleep and your peace? Call on the living Prince of Peace, who will answer when you call to Him. Remember that you can close your eyes and rest because God's eyes never close. The One who never sleeps cares for you personally and watches over you. The same God who created the expanse of the heavens, majestic mountains, glaciers, and everything else on earth and holds the whole world together by His powerful word knows the number of hairs on our heads—and watchfully and lovingly cares about each one of us individually. This one truth is worth rejoicing about all day—the Prince of Peace cares about me! I am of infinite value to Him. Nothing happens to me apart from His knowledge. He knows my name, my aches and struggles, and He loves me. We do not have to be afraid, for our Prince of Peace is watching over us. Our part is to stay connected by trusting Him.

Lord Jesus, thank You for setting apart each of us to know You and for answering when I call to You. Let the smile of Your countenance shine on me this day. Grant me peace in Your presence, even before a turnaround or harvest comes. When the night falls, grant me to "lie down in peace and sleep," for You alone keep me safe. Thank You for Your tender, watchful care. Help me to remember all through the day that you are with me. You know every detail about my life—who I am, what I like, where I go—nothing is hidden from You. Your love for me means more than anything else in this world. May I go about my days with quiet confidence and peace, knowing that I am safe in your hand. In mighty Name Above All Names—Prince of Peace, we pray, amen.

Look Up—meditate on Isaiah 9:6

Look In—as you meditate on Isaiah 9:6 pray to see how you might apply it to your life.

Look Out—as you meditate on Isaiah 9:6 pray to see how you might apply it to your relationships with others.

Notes

Many waters can't quench love, neither can floods drown it. If a man would give all the wealth of his house for love, he would be utterly scorned.

unQuenchable love

SONG OF SOLOMON 8:7

Song of Solomon 8:7

17 Unquenchable Love

Unquenchable Love from Song of Solomon 8:7 …

NASB: "Many waters cannot quench love, Nor will rivers overflow it; If a man were to give all the riches of his house for love, It would be utterly despised."

Amplified: Many waters cannot quench love, neither can floods drown it. If a man would offer all the goods of his house for love, he would be utterly scorned and despised.

TLB: Many waters cannot quench the flame of love, neither can the floods drown it. If a man tried to buy it with everything he owned, he couldn't do it."

The Voice: No amount of water can quench love; a raging flood cannot drown it out. If a person tried to exchange all of his wealth for love, then he would be surely rejected

Young's Literal: Many waters are not able to quench the love, And floods do not wash it away. If one give all the wealth of his house for love, Treading down—they tread upon it.

"Many waters cannot quench (in Hebrew is the word, *kabah,* which means to quench, put out, extinguish) love, Nor will rivers overflow it; If a man were to give all the riches of his house for love, It would be utterly despised."

Pastor Robert Hawker writes: Many waters cannot quench love, neither can the floods drown it: if a man would give all the substance of his house for love, it would utterly be contemned. Here is the same obscurity in this verse, whether the words are principally applicable to Christ or to his Church. If we consider the Church as thus expressing her affection, every believer ought to be enabled to adopt the sentiment contained in them. For as some blessed martyrs in times past have waded not only through waters and floods under the persecutions of the ungodly, but through blood, to testify their love to Jesus; so ought believers in every age. Neither the malice of enemies, nor the slights of friends, the unkindness of relations, and the sneers of the world; the infidelity of men, nor the rage of devils; since none of these can separate from the love of Christ; surely none of them ought to have influence to lessen in our hearts that love. But as it is not to be bought with money, so ought every child of God to prize it above all things. They should despise everything the world holds dear, in order to keep alive the immortal spark, not to be extinguished by the floods or waters of immortal hatred. But if we read the verse with an eye to Christ, the subject contained in it rises in glory. Such indeed was the love of Christ to his Church, that neither the view of his Father's burning anger against sin, nor all the sufferings he had to sustain in his own sacred person, when doing away the evil of sin by the sacrifice of himself, could for one moment make his holy soul remit his love to his redeemed. Yea, if possible, more deeply wounding still to his tender heart, not all the baseness and ingratitude of his redeemed, could extinguish the holy flame of his love. Reader! pause over this subject, and contemplate well the wondrous contents of it, and then say, Is not the love of Christ in the heights and depths, in the breadths and lengths of it, a love of God, which passes knowledge?"

Pastor Adam Clarke writes: "Many waters—Neither common nor uncommon adversities, even of the most ruinous nature, can destroy love when it is pure; and pure love is such that nothing can procure it. If it be not excited naturally, no money can purchase it, no property can procure it, no arts can persuade it. How vain is the thought of old rich men hoping to procure the affections of young women by loading them with presents and wealth! No woman can command her affections; they are not in her power. Where they do not rise spontaneously, they can never exist. "If a man would give all the substance of his house for love, it would be utterly contemned." That is a general truth, applying to all forms of real love; you cannot purchase love. Who, for instance, could purchase a mother s love? Take, again, even the love of friends; I only instance that just to show how true our text is in relation to all forms of love. Rest assured that this is pre-eminently true when we get into higher regions, when we come to think of the love of Jesus, and when we think of that love which springs up in the human breast towards Jesus when the Spirit of God has renewed the heart and shed abroad the love of God within the soul. If a man should offer to give all the substance of his house for either of these forms of love, it would utterly be contemned."

Our fellowship with God is restored through our own repentance and confession. Jesus provided for this through his finished work on the cross. He died so that we would be pardoned and restored to the Father. When we come to Jesus, he forgives our sins of the past, sins of the present, and all the sins we will ever commit in the future. But we who are forgiven much must love and forgive others much! Ask the Holy Spirit to show you any areas where you need to practice forgiveness. God is ready to provide the grace to enable us to forgive and to experience being fully forgiven ourselves.

Lord Jesus, thank You for giving me a forgiving heart. Thank You for Your perfect work on the cross, where Your blood covers me, and I receive Your forgiveness and the gift of being able to forgive those who have wronged me. I never want to cause your presence in my life to be quenched because of unforgiveness. Thank You for creating in me a free and forgiving spirit that sees others as You do, responds to them with Your heart, and prays for them with Your love. In Your mighty Name Above All Names—Unquenchable Love, we pray, amen.

Look Up—meditate on Song of Solomon 8:7

Look In—as you meditate on Song of Solomon 8:7 pray to see how you might apply it to your life.

Look Out—as you meditate on Song of Solomon 8:7 pray to see how you might apply it to your relationships with others.

Why do you seek the living among the dead? He isn't here, but is risen.

Risen Lord
LUKE 24:6

Luke 24:5,6

18 Risen Lord

Risen Lord from Luke 24:6 …

NASB: He is not here, but He has risen. Remember how He spoke to you while He was still in Galilee

Expanded: He is not here; he has risen from the dead. Do you remember what he told you [while he was still] in Galilee?

God's Word: He's not here. He has been brought back to life! Remember what he told you while he was still in Galilee.

TLB: He isn't here! He has come back to life again! Don't you remember what he told you back in Galilee

The Voice: He is not here. He has risen from the dead. Don't you remember what He told you way back in Galilee?

Pastor John MacArthur writes: "The resurrection of Christ is the greatest event in history. It is the main event in God's redemptive plan. It is the cornerstone and foundation of the gospel. According to Romans 10:9-10 in order to be saved you have to believe in the resurrection of Jesus Christ. Now, we understand that the message that God has delivered to sinners throughout all of Scripture is that death does not end our existence. That is the message of Scripture from the start to the finish, that death is merely the doorway into eternity. Every human being ever born will live forever, fully conscious either in everlasting joy or everlasting suffering."

Pastor John MacArthur continues: "There's a beautiful little indication by Luke here that I love. "When they entered, they didn't find the body of the Lord Jesus." They could have said the body of Jesus. Lord Jesus, that is not a title used in the description of the death and burial of Jesus, but it's a title of His by way of resurrection. God raised Him from the dead and declared Him Lord. In fact, that is exactly what Peter said on Pentecost, "Therefore, let all the house of Israel know for certain that God has made Him both Lord and Christ." He is now the Lord. "He has now been given the Name which is above every name, the name Lord, that at that name every knee should bow." "Behold, two men suddenly stood near them in dazzling apparel, like the angel who had come in the darkness when the soldiers were still there and removed the stone," same dazzling appearance. And as the women were terrified and bowed their faces to the ground, the men said to them, "Why do you seek the living one among the dead? He is not here, but He has risen. Remember how He spoke to you while He was still in Galilee saying that the Son of Man must be delivered into the hands of sinful men and be crucified and the third day rise again."

Pastor MacArthur concludes: "The first great evidence of the resurrection is the empty tomb. At first, when the women saw them, verse 4, it says they stood near them. Later, John says when Mary Magdalene came back at a later time she comes back, they were sitting. There's no contradiction there. This again is a very kind of natural scene. Now, they are standing and later they're sitting at the place where Jesus had been lain inside the tomb. They're wearing these dazzling clothes, like the dazzling appearance of Jesus in the transfiguration, the blazing appearance of the saints in Revelation 19 who returned with something of the glory, the *Shekinah* reflection of heaven itself. This is clearly indicating that these are divine messengers. There's no other explanation. They're not just young men. They're not just angels who are men, and you can't tell that they are really angels. They are angels who appear in the form of young men but who are dazzling, blazing, brilliant, shining beings that are obviously heavenly, and the result is predictable, as the women were terrified and bowed their faces to the ground, they are terrified, *emphobos,* an emphatic form of the word *phobos*, from which you get phobia, fear, panic, terror sets in. This, by the way, is the first announcement that Jesus is alive. Why are you seeking the living One? The One who is life, the One who cannot die, the One death cannot hold among the dead. And then the angels get very specific. Verse 6, "He is not here," why? "But He has risen," passive, He has been raised, *ēgerthē*. He has been raised. This is the only possible explanation for the empty tomb, and it is the testimony of God's holy messengers. It is inerrant, it is authoritative, it is irrefutable, and it is a fulfillment of the promise. If you believe in the resurrection, Jesus is therefore Lord. If you don't want Jesus as Lord, then you better deny the resurrection. If there is a resurrection, Jesus is Lord and the Bible is true. And every man is therefore accountable to His lordship. The single greatest evidence of the resurrection is the testimony of God, given by angels from His presence and reiterated by the Spirit of God inspiring the writers of the New Testament."

Biblical scholar and theologian Norval Geldenhuys has said: "If Jesus hadn't risen, the New Testament would never have been written. For who would have taken to write the biography of anyone who had laid tremendous claim to Messiahship and divinity, but whose career terminated in a shameful death? But God be praised, Jesus did arise, and that is why the group of men who wrote the books of the New Testament took up their pens with such enthusiasm and holy conviction. And throughout their writings we perceived the clear note of their firm conviction that Jesus Christ, who had died, rose again from the dead and was invested with divine power and glory."

God so loved the world that he sent his only Son, and yet that Son was met with death and dishonor. His resurrection proved once and for all that He was indeed the Son of God. Every day we cross paths with someone who needs to hear the good news that the Lord saves. We can never fully plumb the depths of God's character and attributes, but with every day and every experience we can discover new facets about God. May we share what the Lord has done in our own lives so that others might be drawn to him. Each of us can purpose to do that. The most powerful evangelism doesn't take place within the four walls of a church building. It occurs as we share with others in our neighborhood and workplace the good news of what God has done for us individually and for the whole world in the life, death, and resurrection of Jesus Christ. Ask God to bring people across your path today who need to hear the good news that God saves and that He loves them. And then ask Him for the compassion and courage to share the reason for your hope and to pray for those people.

Heavenly Father, I rejoice over the resurrection of your precious Son! I won't forget what He has done for me. You sent him to earth and he was dishonored, but I pray that I will honor him by remembering the cross. I will acknowledge His sacrifice and celebrate His resurrection. Thank you that He burst from the tomb to live inside us. Lord Jesus, thank You for giving us life through Your resurrection. Thank You for drawing to Yourself those who need to believe and be saved from sin, and death, and hell, and anticipate the glorious resurrection that awaits those who love Christ. In Your mighty Name Above All Names—Risen Lord, we pray, amen.

Look Up—meditate on Luke 24:6

Look In—as you meditate on Luke 24:6 pray to see how you might apply it to your life.

Look Out—as you meditate on Luke 24:6 pray to see how you might apply it to your relationships with others.

Notes

They said to the woman,
"Now we believe,
not because of your speaking;
for we have heard for ourselves,
and know that this
is indeed the Christ,
the Savior of the world."

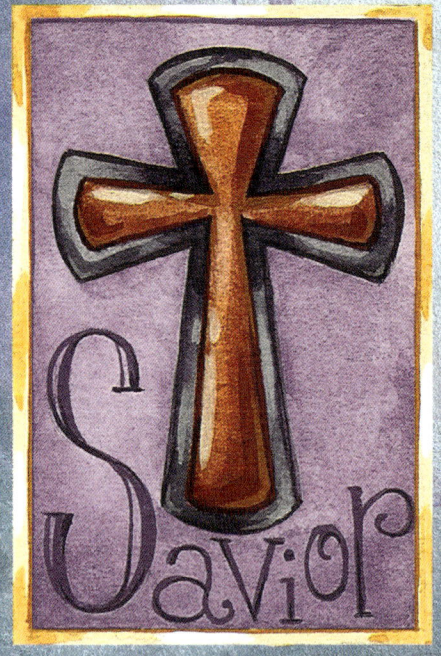

Savior

John 4:42

19 Savior

Savior from John 4:42 …

NASB: and they were saying to the woman, "It is no longer because of what you said that we believe, for we have heard for ourselves and know that this One is indeed the Savior of the world."

Amplified: And they told the woman, Now we no longer believe (trust, have faith) just because of what you said; for we have heard Him ourselves [personally], and we know that He truly is the Savior of the world, the Christ.

Expanded: They said to the woman, "·First we believed in Jesus [It is no longer] because of what you said, but now we believe because we heard him ourselves. We know that this man really is the Savior of the world."

J.B. Phillips: As they told the woman, "We don't believe any longer now because of what you said. We have heard him with our own ears. We know now that this must be the man who will save the world!"

TLB: Then they said to the woman, "Now we believe because we have heard him ourselves, not just because of what you told us. He is indeed the Savior of the world."

Young's Literal: and said to the woman -- `No more because of thy speaking do we believe; for we ourselves have heard and known that this is truly the Savior of the world -- the Christ.'

Bible study teacher Beth Moore writes: "Christ's encounter with the woman at the well introduces us to some realities of life we desperately need to remember: Our insatiable need or craving for too much of anything is symptomatic of unmet needs or "empty places." Salvation does not equal satisfaction. You can be genuinely saved and still be unsatisfied. Satisfaction comes only when every empty place is filled with the fullness of Christ. While salvation comes to us as a gift from God, we find satisfaction in Him as we deliberately surrender all parts of our lives to Him. Though she did not immediately profess her faith, the Samaritan woman later recounted her encounter with Jesus in public, influencing the whole town. Many from the town believed in Jesus because of the woman's testimony. They urged Jesus to stay on and teach them, too. In the end, the townspeople said to the woman, "We no longer believe just because of what you said; now we have heard for ourselves, and we know that this man really is the Savior of the world." How can we share the full message of the Bible, including God's view of sin and the possibility of eternal separation from Him, without driving away our listeners? While this is an important and natural question to ask, we must remember God's promise to draw unbelievers to Himself. Jesus said, "No one can come to me unless the Father who sent me draws him" (John 6:44) Our part in God's work is to love unbelievers and hold out the truth to them. We may not see the results of our sharing. God, however, does see the continuing process in each life. He reveals Himself in His Word and through those who are willing to share His Word and His love with unbelievers. Only He knows how each individual heart responds to Him. We can trust God to do His part perfectly."

Pastor Don Fortner writes: "In Isaiah 43:3, He is Jehovah our God; but more than that, he is Jehovah our Righteousness. The Lord our God is the Lord our Righteousness. Then he declares himself to be "Thy Savior." The Lord our God, who is the Lord our Righteousness, is the Lord our Savior. The Lord who redeemed us, called us, and made us holy by his almighty grace is our Savior. Who is he? What is his name? The answer is found in Matthew 1:21. The angel of the Lord said to Joseph, "She shall bring forth a son, and thou shall call his name Jesus; for he shall save his people from their sins." The Lord our God, Jehovah, is Jesus our Savior. Jesus Christ is Jehovah our God come to save. With the incarnation, life, death, resurrection, and ascension of our Lord Jesus Christ all these names of our God and Savior and the messages contained in them are fulfilled. The name by which the Lord God appeared to his saints in the types and prophecies of the Old Testament is Jehovah. Jesus, the name which our Lord assumed when he came into the earth as a man, is a transliteration of the Old Testament name Joshua, which means "Jehovah is salvation," or "Jehovah is Savior." The name of the God-Man, who is our

Savior is Jehovah-Jesus, or the Lord Jesus; and he is the Christ. Jehovah-Jesus is God over all and blessed forever, Creator and sovereign Ruler of all things He is a real man, touched with the feeling of our infirmities. He knows the temptations of his people in every age and at every stage of life. He knows the pain of loneliness and isolation. He knows the bitterness of scornful and mocking jeers. He knows the grief of betrayal by friends. He knows the weakness of hunger and the fever of sickness. He knows the sorrows of bereavement, sin, and death. Though he had no sin of his own and consequently no sorrow of his own, when he came to be made sin for us he suffered for us all the consequences of sin. Child of God, be assured that whatever it is that touches you, it has touched him. He knows what you feel. He knows the pain that crushes your heart which no one else can understand. What is your trouble? What is your sorrow? What is your burden? Tell it to Jehovah-Jesus. He is a friend who understands and a God who is able to help. He not only knows our weaknesses and needs, he is able to do something about them. Jehovah-Jesus is our Mediator, our Savior, our Brother, our Advocate, and our God. The angel did not say, "He shall reward his people for their righteousness." He did not say, "He shall save his people from becoming sinners." He said, "He shall save his people from their sins." The connecting link between Christ and his people is not their goodness, but their sins. Christ never gave himself for our righteousness. He gave himself for our sins. If we had never sinned we would never have needed a Savior. Had we never sinned, the name of Jesus would never have been heard. "The first link between my soul and Christ is, not my goodness, but my badness; not my merit, but my misery; not my standing, but my falling; not my riches, but my need" (C.H. Spurgeon).

Rather than wait for the unbeliever to come to church, Christ brought a living gospel to the doorstep of their homes. The challenge is no less compelling today. Right outside the walls of your local church are people who are seeking answers. There are those who need healing, who are lonely, and who may even be reviled by others in their community. You have good medicine to dispense—a gospel message that heals hearts and changes lives and reconciles sinners to a merciful Savior—Jesus Christ.

Lord Jesus, thank You for giving me a faith in You that is real and personal. You come to those of us who know that apart from You we are sick, instead of to those who believe that they are well, but are really sick at heart. Thank You for being my Great Physician and for never being too busy to attend to my needs or wounds. Guide me in joyfully dispensing to others the good medicine you pour out to me. There are so many who don't know you and need to hear the truth. Help me to share my faith in such a way that others will be drawn to you and will accept you as their Savior. In Your mighty Name Above All Names—Savior, we pray, amen.

Look Up—meditate on John 4:42

Look In—as you meditate on John 4:42 pray to see how you might apply it to your life.

Look Out—as you meditate on John 4:42 pray to see how you might apply it to your relationships with others.

Notes

Truth
John 14:6

I am the way the truth, and the life. No one comes to the Father, except through Me. He who has seen Me has seen the Father.

John 14:6, 9

20 Truth

Truth from John 14:6 …

NASB: Jesus *said to him, "I am the way, and the truth, and the life; no one comes to the Father but through Me.

Amplified: Jesus said to him, "I am the [only] Way [to God] and the [real] Truth and the [real] Life; no one comes to the Father but through Me.

Expanded: Jesus answered, "I am ·the way, and the truth, and the life [or the one true way to have life]. ·The only way to the Father is through me [L No one comes to the Father except through me].

J. B. Phillips: "I myself am the road," replied Jesus, "and the truth and the life. No one approaches the Father except through me."

The Message: Jesus said, "I am the Road, also the Truth, also the Life. No one gets to the Father apart from me."

Pastor F. B. Meyer writes: "I am the Way," said our Lord. Each day, as we leave our home, we know that the prepared path lies before us, in the good works which God has prepared for us to walk in. And when we are ignorant of their direction, and are at a loss as to where to place our steps, we have only to concern ourselves with Christ, and almost unconsciously we shall find ourselves making progress in the destined way. Christ is the Way: love Christ, trust Christ, obey Christ, be concerned with Christ, and all else will be added. Christ is the Way. When the heart is wrapped up in Him, it is on the way, and it is making progress, although it never counts the rate or distance, so occupied is it with Him. To be wrapped up in the love of Christ is to make ever deeper discoveries into the heart of God. He is the Way to God: to know Him is to come to the Father. We fully know truth only as it is in Jesus. When the Spirit of Truth would lead us into all truth, He can do nothing better than take of the things of Christ, and reveal them to us, because to know Christ is to know the truth in its most complete, most convenient, and most accessible form. If you know Christ intimately and fully, even if you know nothing else, you will know the truth, and the truth will make you free. If you love truth, and are a child of the truth, you will be inevitably attracted to Christ, and recognize the truth that speaks through his glorious nature. Distinguish between Christ the Truth, and truth about Him. Many true things may be said about Him; but we are not saved by truths about Him, but by Himself, the Truth. To know Him is to be at the fountain-head of all truth; and the soul which has dwelt with Him by day and night will find itself not only inspired by an undying love for the true, but able to hold fellowship with truth-lovers and truth-seekers everywhere; nay, will be able even to instruct those who have the reputation of great learning and knowledge in the schools of human thought. "I give eternal life unto my sheep," He said, "and they shall never perish." "He that believeth on the Son hath eternal life." If, then, you are wanting life, and life more abundantly, you must have Christ. Do not seek it, but Him: not the stream, but the fountain; not the word, but the speaker; not the fruit, but the tree. He is the Life and Light of men. And if you have Christ, you have life. You may not be competent to define or analyze it; you may not be able to specify the place or time when it first broke into your soul; you may hardly be able to distinguish it from the workings of your own life: but if you have Christ, trust Christ, desire Christ above all, you have the Life. "I," said Jesus, "am the Way, the Truth, and the Life."

Pastor John Gill writes: "Christ is not merely the way, as he goes before his people as an example; or merely as a prophet, pointing out unto them by his doctrine the way of salvation; but he is the way of salvation itself by his obedience and sacrifice; nor is there any other; he is the way of his Father's appointing, and which is entirely agreeable to the perfections of God, and suitable to the case and condition of sinners; he is the way to all the blessings of the covenant of grace; and he is the right way into a Gospel church state here; no one comes rightly into a church of Christ but by faith in him; and he is the way to heaven: he is entered into it himself by his own blood, and has opened the way to it through himself for his people: he adds, he is not only true, but truth itself: this may regard his person and character; he is the true God, and eternal life; truly and really man; as a prophet he taught the way of God in truth; as a priest, he is a faithful, as well as a merciful one, true and faithful to him that appointed him; and as a King, just and true are all his ways and administrations: he is the sum and substance of all the truths of the Gospel; they are all full of him, and center in him; and he is the truth of all the types and shadows, promises and prophecies of the Old Testament; they have all their accomplishment in him; and he is the true way, in opposition to all false ones of man's devising. Christ is the author and giver of life, natural, spiritual, and eternal.'

Pastor Wil Pounds writes: "Jesus Christ is the full, final, and complete revelation of God. Jesus is the truth. "I myself am the truth." "I and I alone, and no one else am the truth." Jesus is the actual embodiment of the truth. He is the authoritative representative and revealer of God. He hears what the Father says and does what the Father tells Him to do (5:19; 8:29). You can paraphrase John 14:6, "I am the way that reveals the truth (about God) and gives life (to people)." Jesus Christ is the very reality of all God's grace toward us sinners. Grace and truth could not merely be given. It actually came through the living person of Jesus Christ. The truth is found in the person of Jesus Christ. He is the truth. Truth is God's very reality revealing itself in Jesus. Truth is knowledge of God through Jesus Christ. To have the Truth is to have eternal life (17:3). Have you humbled yourself and bowed down before Him who is the Truth—eternal Truth? The emphasis in this great statement is not just truth as opposed to a lie, reality as opposed to mere illusion, but His faithfulness, reliability, trustworthiness, sureness. Jesus Christ is the "God of truth" (Ps. 31:5; Isa. 65:16). Absolute truth is characteristic of God, and it is only as we know God that we know truth. It includes the complete reliability and the complete integrity of God. He will certainly act in accordance with the highest conceivable integrity and righteousness. The emphasis is on the fact that you can know Him so clearly that it may be said you see Him. The work of the Holy Spirit is to take the things of Christ and show them to the believer. Do you seek the truth? "Believe Me that I am in the Father, and the Father in Me" (v. 11). "Believe that the Father is in Me and I in Him" (10:38). What is our response? "And we know that the Son of God has come, and has given us understanding so that we may know Him who is true; and we are in Him who is true, in His Son Jesus Christ. This is the true God and eternal life" (1 John 5:20). Jesus Christ is the way, the truth and the life."

Pastor John MacArthur writes: "Jesus says , "I am the way, the truth, and the life." We don't need to know how to get to heaven; Jesus is coming to get us. We are to trust Him. He is the way. When the right time comes, He will take us by the hand and lead us right to the Father's house. If you were to go into a strange town and ask for directions, it would be better if someone told you to follow him instead of having him explain how to get to your destination. That's what Jesus is going to do. Instead of giving us directions, He will take us to the Father's house. Don't worry about what will happen at death or the Rapture. Jesus will come back for you. Do you trust Him in death? Do you trust Him? What if you die, do you trust Him? Are you ready to just die and He'll just take you? Do you believe Him for that? He says to those disciples, "Trust Me, I'll bring you. Trust Me, Jesus says, "You don't need a map, I'm the way, the truth and the life. I am the way to the Father, I am the truth whether in this world or the world to come. I am the life that is eternal. It's all in Christ. He's everything a man needs. Everything Adam lost, you regain in Jesus Christ. Trust Me, trust My presence, trust My promises, trust My person, I'm the way. No matter how bad it looks, there's comfort because you can trust Him. Jesus then finished off this statement by saying this, "And no man cometh unto the Father but by Me." You may have heard about heaven and about the comfort that comes by trusting Christ, but you will never be there, you will never go there because the only way to get there is through faith in Jesus Christ and you've never put your faith in Jesus Christ. Disaster of all disasters. "No man cometh unto the Father but by Me." Don't take another breath until you've invited Jesus Christ to come into your life to be your Savior and your escort into the presence of the Father."

Heavenly Father, we thank You for teaching us trust. We thank You that Jesus Christ is so worthy of our trust. We want to tell You we trust You. Thank You for comforting us with these words. Thank You for saying You'd always be with us, Your presence. Thank You for the promise that You're up there getting it ready for us. Thank You for the wonderful fact of Your person, that You are the way that after we die and leave this world or are taken in the Rapture, You're our personal escort. We don't need to have a chart or a map, You're the way, You're the truth and You're the life. We thank You for that. Thank you for your wonder-working power! I once was locked in a prison of darkness to Your truth and light. Thank You for shining the light of Your truth into my heart and freeing me from sin. Please use me to share the truth about Your great power with others who need to know true freedom in Christ. In Your mighty Name Above All Names—the Way, the Truth, and the Life, we pray, amen.

Look Up—meditate on John 14:6

Look In—as you meditate on John 14:6 pray to see how you might apply it to your life.

Look Out—as you meditate on John 14:6 pray to see how you might apply it to your relationships with others.

Notes

His Son is the radiance
of His glory,
the very image of His substance,
and upholding all things
by the word of His power,
when He had made purification for sins,
sat down on the right hand
of the Majesty on high.

Upholder of
HEBREWS 1:3
all things

Hebrews 1:3

21 Upholder of All Things

Upholder of All Things from Hebrews 1:3 …

NASB: And He is the radiance of His glory and the exact representation of His nature, and upholds all things by the word of His power. When He had made purification of sins, He sat down at the right hand of the Majesty on high.

Amplified: He is the sole expression of the glory of God [the Light-being, the out-raying or radiance of the divine], and He is the perfect imprint and very image of [God's] nature, upholding and maintaining and guiding and propelling the universe by His mighty word of power. When He had by offering Himself accomplished our cleansing of sins and riddance of guilt, He sat down at the right hand of the divine Majesty on high.

ESV: He is the radiance of the glory of God and the exact imprint of his nature, and he upholds the universe by the word of his power. After making purification for sins, he sat down at the right hand of the Majesty on high.

J. B. Phillips: God, who gave our forefathers many different glimpses of the truth in the words of the prophets, has now, at the end of the present age, given us the truth in the Son. Through the Son God made the whole universe, and to the Son he has ordained that all creation shall ultimately belong. This Son, radiance of the glory of God, flawless expression of the nature of God, himself the upholding principle of all that is, effected in person the reconciliation between God and man and then took his seat at the right hand of the majesty on high.

Wuest: Who, being the out-raying [effulgence] of His glory and the exact reproduction of His essence, and sustaining, guiding, and propelling all things by the word of His power, having made purification of sins, sat down on the right hand of the Majesty on high.

Young's Literal: who being the brightness of the glory, and the impress of His subsistence, bearing up also the all things by the saying of his might -- through himself having made a cleansing of our sins, sat down at the right hand of the greatness in the highest.

Greek Scholar Kenneth Wuest writes: "The word substance deserves careful treatment. In Greek, it is *hupostasis*, made up of stasis "to stand," and *hupo* "under," meaning "that which stands under, a foundation." It speaks of the ground on which one builds a hope. Moulton and Milligan's Vocabulary of the Greek New Testament report its use as a legal term. They say that it stands for "the whole body of documents bearing on the ownership of a person's property, deposited in archives, and forming the evidence of ownership." They suggest the translation, "Faith is the title-deed of things hoped for." The Holy Spirit energized act of faith which a believer exercises in the Lord Jesus is the title-deed which God puts in his hand, guaranteeing to him the possession of the thing for which he trusted Him. Thus, he would have assurance. Theologian Marvin Vincent translates, "Faith is the assurance of things hoped for." He says that "It is the firm grasp of faith on unseen fact."

Pastor Charles Spurgeon writes: "Whatever God is, Christ is. The very likeness of God, the very Godhead of Godhead, the very Deity of Deity, is in Christ Jesus. Dr. John Owen, who loves to explain the spiritual meaning in the Letter to the Hebrews by the types in the Old Testament, explains the brightness of the Father's glory by a reference to the Shekinah over the mercy seat, which was the only visible token of the presence of God there. An extraordinary brightness is said to have shone forth from between the cherubim. Now, Christ is God manifesting Himself in His brightness. But, on his forehead, the high priest wore a golden plate, upon which was deeply engraved, in Hebrew letters, the inscription, "Holiness to [or of] Yahweh." Dr. Owen thinks there is a reference, in this "representation of his essence"—this cut-out inscription of God, as it were—to that which was on the forehead of the high priest, and which represented the glorious wholeness or holiness of Yahweh, which is His great glory. You see how glorious was His original—the "representation" of His Father's person. How lowly did He become to purge away our sins, and that by Himself, too, using His own body to be the means, by His sufferings, of taking away our guilt. Not by proxy did He serve us, but by Himself. Oh, this is wondrous love!"

Pastor Vernon C. Grounds provides two wonderful illustrations for Hebrews 1:3 : "A Navy pilot was describing his complex helicopter to his parents one day. He told them that a small hexagonal nut held the main rotor to the mast of the helicopter. "Guess what we call that nut?" he asked his mother. She could only shrug her shoulders. With a smile, the pilot answered his own question: "It's called a Jesus nut." That may sound irreverent, but here's an explanation. If that small piece of metal ever came off, the helicopter would not be able to stay in the air but would come crashing to the ground. So it's understandable why pilots in the Vietnam War gave that little part the name "Jesus nut." The writer to the Hebrews said that Jesus, who made the world, upholds "all things by the word of His power" (Hebrews 1:3). Because of Him, we inhabit a created cosmos, not a chaotic accident. He who made all reality keeps it from collapsing. We also need Jesus Christ as our Savior from sin and as Lord of our everyday lives. He is the One who can lift us above the degrading forces of evil in our world. If you feel as if your life is crashing down around you, remember that it's Jesus who holds all things together—even your life. "Why don't the stars fall down?" A child may ask that question, but so does an astronomer. And they both get essentially the same answer: A mysterious power or energy upholds everything and prevents our cosmos from collapsing into chaos. Hebrews 1:3 tells us that it is Jesus who upholds all things by the word of His power. He is the source of all the energy there is, whether the explosive potential packed inside an atom or the steaming kettle on the kitchen stove. That energy is not simply a mindless force. No, God is the personal power who created everything out of nothing, including the stars. So when life's problems are baffling, when you face some impossibility, call upon the wonder-working God who upholds all things. And remember that with our almighty God, nothing is impossible."

Maybe, like me, you've been on an airplane as it flew through a thunderstorm. All around you, you see and hear the storm's beating rain and the wind whipping against the cabin wall. Looks of worry and panic cloud passengers' faces as we wonder when will we get to the other side of the storm. We long to see the sun, and as soon as the plane has landed, we quickly form a line to get off. On such a turbulent flight we can dramatically experience the light and peace after a storm almost instantly. Peace replaces anxiety in just a moment as we break through a cloud and see the sun and its radiance just on the other side of the storm. As God's children we do not need to wait until our personal storms have passed in order to see and experience the radiance, the substance, the light and peace of the Son—the Upholder of All Things. The Word of God, His truth, not only sustains us in the storms of life, but opens our eyes to see the Son, the exact representation of His nature, the radiance of God's glory, while we are soaring through them.

Lord Jesus, Upholder of All Things, I want to know You and Your will. I'm willing to be willing to surrender to Your will. No matter what storms of life I may face, I will keep my eyes on the brightness of Jesus Christ, Your Son—the radiance of your glory! Help me to look to You and to trust in You today. There is great joy to be found in living with my eyes fixed on You. Help me to do that so that my life will be radiant with Your joy. May others be drawn to You because of the radiance and joy You have put in my heart. In Your mighty Name Above All Names—Upholder of All Things, we pray, amen.

Look Up—meditate on Hebrews 1:3

Look In—as you meditate on Hebrews 1:3 pray to see how you might apply it to your life.

Look Out—as you meditate on Hebrews 1:3 pray to see how you might apply it to your relationships with others.

Notes

I am the vine.
You are the branches.
He who remains in Me
and I in him
bears much fruit.

the true Vine
John 15:5

John 15:5

22 The True Vine

The True Vine from John 15:5 …

NASB: "I am the vine, you are the branches; he who abides in Me and I in him, he bears much fruit, for apart from Me you can do nothing.

Amplified: I am the Vine; you are the branches. Whoever lives in Me and I in him bears much (abundant) fruit. However, apart from Me [cut off from vital union with Me] you can do nothing.

J. B. Phillips: I am the vine itself, you are the branches. It is the man who shares my life and whose life I share who proves fruitful. For the plain fact is that apart from me you can do nothing at all.

TLB: Yes, I am the Vine; you are the branches. Whoever lives in me and I in him shall produce a large crop of fruit. For apart from me you can't do a thing.

The Message: I am the Vine, you are the branches. When you're joined with me and I with you, the relation intimate and organic, the harvest is sure to be abundant. Separated, you can't produce a thing.

Pastor John MacArthur writes: "The night before His death, Jesus says, "I am the Vine." Like the other great "I am" passages recorded in the Gospel of John, it points to His deity. Each one is a metaphor that elevates Jesus to the level of Creator, Sustainer, Savior, and Lord—titles that can be claimed only by God. The metaphor in John 15 is of a vine and its branches. The vine is the source and sustenance of life for the branches, and the branches must abide in the vine to live and bear fruit. Jesus, of course, is the vine, and the branches are people. The true meaning of the metaphor is made clear when we consider the characters in that night's drama. The disciples were with Jesus. He had loved them to the uttermost; He had comforted them with the words in John chapter 14. The Father was foremost in His thoughts, because He was thinking of the events of the next day. Jesus made a promise to His children, "I give eternal life to them, and they will never perish; and no one will snatch them out of My hand." He guaranteed the security of the child of God: "All that the Father gives Me will come to Me, and the one who comes to Me I will certainly not cast out." A true believer cannot lose his salvation and be condemned to hell. A branch that is truly connected to the vine is secure and will never be removed. Jesus chose the figure of a vine for several reasons. The lowliness of a vine demonstrates His humility. It also pictures a close, permanent, vital union between the vine and branches. It is symbolic of belonging, because branches belong entirely to the vine; if branches are to live and bear fruit, they must completely depend on the vine for nourishment, support, strength, and vitality. Yet many who call themselves Christians fail to depend on Christ. Instead of being attached to the true vine, they are tied to a bank account. Others are attached to their education. Some have tried to make vines out of popularity, fame, personal skills, possessions, relationships, or fleshly desires. But none of those things can sustain or bear fruit. The true vine is Christ."

Pastor Ray Stedman writes: Jesus does not leave the interpretation up to us. He identifies what this rich symbolism means. "I am the vine," he says, "the true one." In the words, "I am the true vine," Jesus is not saying that Israel was a false vine. What he means is that he is the true vine of which the nation was a symbol, a picture. It is he who will produce at last the fruit that God was looking for through the centuries. "My Father," Jesus declares, "is the gardener." He is the "vinedresser," the gardener who takes care of the vineyard. Jesus says, "I am the vine, you are the branches." He did not say, "I am the vine, try to be the branches." In other words, He wants us to realize that we are already the branches. We do not have to struggle to become the branches. As His branches, we only have to abide or remain in Christ our vine. How do we do that? We do that by simply being conscious every day of our position in Christ. Because we have received Christ, we are in Christ and are accepted in the Beloved. (2 Corinthians 5:17, Ephesians 1:6) God accepts us because we are in the Beloved and He is in us. And that is how God sees us today when we come into His presence. What the devil wants to do then is to get you to focus on your condition instead of your position in Christ. The devil wants you to focus on your condition and forget your position—that you are the righteousness of God in Christ and that you are seated with Him in heavenly places at the Father's right hand. (2 Corinthians 5:21, Ephesians 2:6) He wants you to forget that you are an heir of God and a joint heir with Christ. (Romans 8:17) The devil knows that once you focus on your position in Christ, it will give you the power to change your condition and circumstances. John 15:5 says that you will bear "much fruit." This means that when you pray against any lack, abundant supply will flow. None of these things can happen by your own doing, but by His life which flows through you. Just as sap flowing through the branches of a vine will cause them to bring forth fruit, His life flowing through you will bring forth a bountiful harvest of provision. You only need to remain conscious of who you are in Christ!"

Oh that we would delight in abiding in Christ, that his Word would be continually in our thoughts, and that we would bear fruit in each season of our lives. None of this happens apart from God's Spirit and power working within us. But fruit bearing is the inevitable by-product of opening our hearts and lives to the power of his life within us. As we abide in Christ and his Word, our roots to go down deep in Christ, keeping us close to him, just as the roots of trees planted along the riverbank sink into the water source so that their leaves stay green and don't wither. And when we pray, the Spirit releases this wonder-working power that draws us to God, roots us deeper in him, and causes our faith to mature. Be assured of God's promise that as you draw near to him today and each day in the year ahead, he will draw near to you.

Lord Jesus, Thank You for being my True Vine, by Your Spirit, give me the desire to read your Word and to meditate on it day and night. Most of all, empower me to do what it says. And for the fruit that is borne, I will give you all the glory! Grant me the power to understand the limitless extent of Your love. Be the center of my life and reveal Yourself to me today! Thank You for Your abundant supply day by day as I abide in you. Thank you for making Your divine wisdom available to me through your indwelling Holy Spirit! Give me a heart which focuses on my position in Christ. I cannot do this on my own. But in your Spirit's power, as Your life flows through me, just as sap flowing through the branches of a vine will cause them to bring forth fruit, enable me to be aware of Your presence with me continually in Christ. In Your mighty Name Above All Names—the True Vine, we pray, amen.

Look Up—meditate on John 15:5

Look In—as you meditate on John 15:5 pray to see how you might apply it to your life.

Look Out—as you meditate on John 15:5 pray to see how you might apply it to your relationships with others.

That which was from the beginning, which we have heard, which we have seen with our eyes, which we have looked upon, and our hands have handled, of the Word of Life.

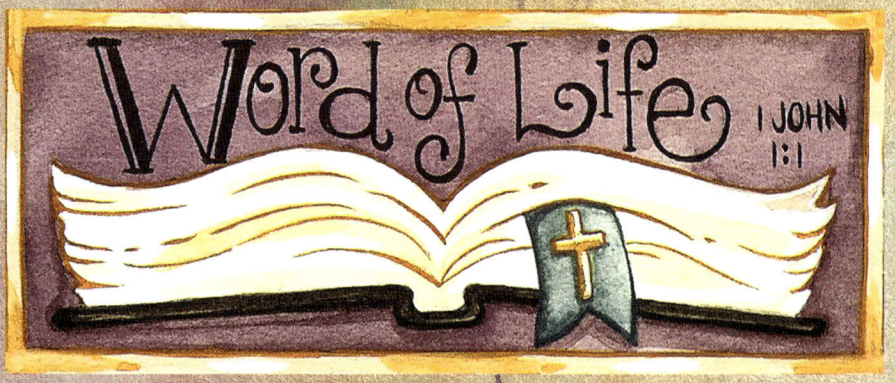

Word of Life — 1 John 1:1

1 John 1:1

23 Word of Life

Word of Life from I John 1:1...

NASB: What was from the beginning, what we have heard, what we have seen with our eyes, what we have looked at and touched with our hands, concerning the Word of Life.

Amplified: [WE ARE writing] about the Word of Life [in] Him Who existed from the beginning, Whom we have heard, Whom we have seen with our [own] eyes, Whom we have gazed upon [for ourselves] and have touched with our [own] hands.

ESV: That which was from the beginning, which we have heard, which we have seen with our eyes, which we looked upon and have touched with our hands, concerning the word of life.

KJV: That which was from the beginning, which we have heard, which we have seen with our eyes, which we have looked upon, and our hands have handled, of the Word of life.

NLT: We proclaim to you the one who existed from the beginning,* whom we have heard and seen. We saw him with our own eyes and touched him with our own hands. He is the Word of life.

J. B. Phillips: We are writing to you about something which has always existed yet which we ourselves actually saw and heard: something which we had an opportunity to observe closely and even to hold in our hands, and yet, as we know now, was something of the very Word of life himself!

Young's Literal: That which was from the beginning, that which we have heard, that which we have seen with our eyes, that which we did behold, and our hands did handle, concerning the Word of the Life.

Pastor John Piper writes: "This is the best commentary on the first phrase of I John 1:1 …"That which was from the beginning..." "From the beginning" means, Christ our Life was when creation began. He is eternal. He had no beginning. He will have no ending. He is not part of creation. In the beginning He is the source of creation. All life comes from Him. He is the spring, not part of the river. "In the beginning was the Word, and the Word was with God and the Word was God. He was in the beginning with God; all things were made through him, and without him was not anything made that was made"

Pastor Marvin Vincent writes: "The phrase *"ho logos tes zoes"*, the Word of the Life, occurs nowhere else in the New Testament. Though the phrase, the Word of the Life, does not elsewhere occur in a personal sense, I incline to regard its primary reference as personal, from the obvious connection of the thought with I John 1:1…"In the beginning was the Word, — in Him was life." In Christ life as the subject, and life as the character of the revelation, were absolutely united."

Word from the Greek logos which means to speak with words; logic, logical, it means something said and describes a communication whereby the mind finds expression in words. *Lógos* then is a general term for speaking, but always used for speaking with rational content. *Lógos* is a word uttered by the human voice which embodies an underlying concept or idea. When one has spoken the sum total of their thoughts concerning something, they have given to their hearer a total concept of that thing. Thus the word *lógos* conveys the idea of "a total concept" of anything. Lógos means the word or outward form by which the inward thought is expressed and made known. It can also refer to the inward thought or reason itself. Note then that *lógos* does not refer merely to a part of speech but to a concept or idea. In other words, in classical Greek, *lógos* never meant just a word in the grammatical sense as the mere name of a thing, but rather the thing referred to, the material, not the formal part.

Pastor John Phillips writes: "The Word! Thoughts remain invisible and inaudible until they are clothed in words. With words, what we think and feel and are can be known. And just as our words reveal us, so, too, the Lord Jesus, as "the Word of life," clothes and reveals the great thoughts and feelings of God regarding our sin and our salvation."

Author Dorothy Sayers writes: "[God] can exact nothing from man that He has not exacted from Himself. He has Himself gone through the whole of human experience, from the trivial irritations of family life and the cramping restrictions of hard work and lack of money to the worst horrors of pain and humiliation, defeat, despair, and death. When He was a man, He played the man. He was born in poverty and died in disgrace and thought it well worthwhile. The incarnation of Jesus Christ is the irrefutable proof that God will do anything to draw near to us."

St. Augustine said, "[God] gave Himself for a time to be handled by the hands of men." We have the written record of John, a man who actually did touch Him. We can trust his account—and we can trust that God wants to be near to you and me.

The same God who created the expanse of the heavens, majestic mountains, glaciers, and everything else on earth and holds the whole world together by his powerful word knows the number of hairs on our heads—and watchfully and lovingly cares about each one of us individually. This one truth is worth rejoicing about all day—God cares about me! I am of infinite value to him. Nothing happens to me apart from his knowledge. He knows my name, my aches and struggles, and he loves me. We do not have to be afraid, for our heavenly Father is watching over us. Our part is to stay connected by trusting him.

Lord Jesus, the Word of Life, thank You for Your tender, watchful care. Help me to remember all through the day that You are with me. You know every detail about my life—who I am, what I like, where I go—nothing is hidden from you. I rejoice because I have no need to be afraid. Your love for me means more than anything else in this world. May I go about my days with quiet confidence and peace, knowing that I am safe in Your hand. Thank You, Lord, for the assurance Your Word gives me that you reign over heaven and earth and that no one can thwart your plans for my life—and for the whole world. I put my trust in You today. Only You understand everything—even those things that are mysteries to me. Because You have all authority on earth and in heaven, I can rest in You. When I am afraid, I trust in You, and I praise you for the sustaining power of your Word. Help me to lay hold of your words to me, for they alone bring me life, health, and peace. Thank You for the gift of Your Word, which comforts, inspires, and guides my path each day. In Your mighty Name Above All Names—the Word of Life, we pray, amen.

Look Up—meditate on I John 1:1

Look In—as you meditate on I John 1:1 pray to see how you might apply it to your life.

Look Out—as you meditate on I John 1:1 pray to see how you might apply it to your relationships with others.

Notes

The God of our fathers raised up Jesus... God exalted Him with His right hand to be a Prince and a Savior, to give repentance to Israel, and remission of sins.

eXalted one
ACTS 5:30,31

Acts 5:30,31

24 Exalted One

Exalted One from Acts 5:30, 31...

NASB: The God of our fathers raised up Jesus, whom you had put to death by hanging Him on a cross. He is the one whom God exalted to His right hand as a Prince and a Savior, to grant repentance to Israel, and forgiveness of sins.

Amplified: The God of our forefathers raised up Jesus, Whom you killed by hanging Him on a tree (cross). God exalted Him to His right hand to be Prince and Leader and Savior and Deliverer and Preserver, in order to grant repentance to Israel and to bestow forgiveness and release from sins.

Expanded: You killed [murdered] Jesus by hanging him on a cross [tree]. But God, the God of our ancestors, raised Jesus up from the dead! Jesus is the One whom God raised [exalted] to be on his right side [hand], as Leader [Prince; Ruler] and Savior. Through him, the people of Israel [Israel] could ·change their hearts and lives [repent] and have their sins forgiven.

J. B. Phillips: It was the God of our fathers who raised up Jesus, whom you murdered by hanging him on a cross of wood. God has raised this man to his own right hand as prince and savior, to bring repentance and the forgiveness of sins to Israel.

Pastor John MacArthur writes: "The God of our fathers raised up Jesus whom ye slew and hanged on a tree." Peter got right back in that Sanhedrin and said, "Right. That's exactly what you did, you slew Him and hanged Him on a tree." The one that God raised up as your Messiah, you hanged on a tree. That word slew is an interesting word that's used only one other time in the New Testament, very unusual word. It means to murder with your own hands. So he says, "You not only slew Him but you hanged Him on a tree." Why does he say that? Well He was crucified. He could have said that, but to say hanged on a tree ties it in with Deuteronomy 21:23. The Old Testament said, "Cursed is anybody who hangs on a tree." That was the most shameful, despicable, cursed death a man could die, and they chose that one for the Son of God. After indictment there is always exaltation of Christ as Messiah, verse 31. "Him hath God exalted with His right hand." Right hand means power. God by power ripped Christ out of the grave and exalted Him and made Him a Prince and a Savior. Now you thought He was nothing. You thought He was something to be trampled, but God lifted Him up and made Him better than a Prince. The Greek word is *Archegos*, which means King, Pioneer. It's got so many meanings…Creator, Originator, Author. All of those words, *Archegos*, has so many concepts. Peter was a fisherman. Maybe one concept that we haven't talked about that Peter may have had in mind is this: on each ship there was a strong swimmer, who was called the *Archegos*. Whenever the ship got into trouble, his job was with a rope around his waist to dive in, swim to shore, secure the rope and then everybody else could get to shore on the rope. But the *Archegos*, was the guy who had to make his way there and secure the rope. He says Jesus Christ is the one who having been killed on this earth when the ship wrecked God lifted Him up, took Him to heaven, He left the rope there and all of us are able to reach it on the basis of His provision. And so Jesus Christ is the Archegos—the strong swimmer who secured the anchor to God and then the Savior who gathers us and takes us into God's presence. At the end of verse 31, "He offered you repentance and forgiveness and beloved there's no forgiveness for a man apart from repentance. That's the missing ingredient so much in the message of salvation. People always talk about salvation and they leave out repentance. That doesn't mean you become sinless. That means you're sorry for your sin and you say, "God help me and make me different." Forgive me, and He does. He is Prince and Savior."

Pastor John Piper writes: "The Foundational Facts of Christianity from Peter's message here in Acts 5:30, 31…

Fact #1—God raised Jesus Christ from the dead. Verse 30: "The God of our fathers raised Jesus whom you killed by hanging him on a tree." The God who created the world—and called Abraham, Isaac, and Israel to be his people—this ever-living God raised Jesus from the dead.

Fact #2—God exalted Jesus to his right hand as Prince and Savior. Verse 31: "God exalted him at his right hand as Leader [or Prince] and Savior." God did not raise Jesus from the dead just to die again. He raised him to reign and to save. He is alive today. He upholds the universe by the word of his power (Hebrews 1:3). All authority in heaven and earth has been given to him (Matthew 28:18). He is building his church as he said he would (Matthew 16:18).

Fact #3—Jesus has authority to give repentance and forgiveness of sins and he is giving them to men and women from all the peoples. Verse 31b: "God exalted him at his right hand as Leader and Savior, to give repentance to Israel and forgiveness of sins." But not only to Israel—that was only the springboard to the world. Acts 11:18 says the church glorified God saying, "Then to the Gentiles [i.e., the peoples] also God has granted repentance unto life."

Our Lord and Savior Jesus Christ is high and holy, the glorious, exalted One. He reigns over all in heaven and on earth. Our Savior needs no house, for His dwelling place is all eternity. And yet He chooses to dwell with—literally to abide and make his home in—those who are anything but "high and holy" and who know it. Rather they are those whose spirits are humble, contrite, open, and teachable. They know how unworthy they are of God's love and mercy. But God's holy and loving heart is moved by individuals who humble themselves and acknowledge their weakness and dependence on him. Then He refreshes, revives, and gives new courage to these repentant souls. How gracious our God is!

Lord Jesus, You are high and lifted up, glorious and exalted! And I am not. I bow before You and ask You to develop in me a heart of humility. Thank You for meeting me right where I am and for bringing renewed courage for my life. Thank you for the ministry you have entrusted to me. If others praise me, help me to remember that my one purpose should be that Your gospel is proclaimed and You are exalted. In everything I do, may I be a stepping-stone instead of a stumbling block so that others may come to know you as Savior and Lord. In Your mighty Name Above All Names—Exalted One, we pray, amen.

Look Up—meditate on Acts 5:30, 31

Look In—as you meditate on Acts 5:30, 31 pray to see how you might apply it to your life.

Look Out—as you meditate on Acts 5:30, 31 pray to see how you might apply it to your relationships with others.

Moses said to God, "Behold, when I come to the children of Israel, and tell them, 'The God of your fathers has sent me to you,' and they ask me, 'What is his name?' what should I tell them?"

God said to Moses,
"I AM WHO I AM"

..."You shall tell the children of Israel this, 'Yahweh, the God of your fathers, the God of Abraham, the God of Isaac, and the God of Jacob, has sent me to you.'

This is my name forever, and this is my memorial to all generations."

Exodus 3:13,15

25 Yahweh

Yahweh from Exodus 3:13,15…

HCSB: Then Moses asked God, "If I go to the Israelites and say to them: The God of your fathers has sent me to you, and they ask me, 'What is His name?' what should I tell them?" God also said to Moses, "Say this to the Israelites: Yahweh, the God of your fathers, the God of Abraham, the God of Isaac, and the God of Jacob, has sent me to you. This is My name forever; this is how I am to be remembered in every generation."

LEB: But Moses said to God, "Look, if I go to the Israelites and I say to them, 'The God of your ancestors has sent me to you,' and they say to me, 'What is his name?' then what shall I say to them?" And God said again to Moses, "So you must say to the Israelites, 'Yahweh, the God of your ancestors, the God of Abraham, the God of Isaac, and the God of Jacob, has sent me to you. This is my name forever, and this is my remembrance from generation to generation.'"

NOG: Then Moses replied to Elohim, "Suppose I go to the people of Israel and say to them, 'The Elohim of your ancestors has sent me to you,' and they ask me, 'What is his name?' What should I tell them?" Again Elohim said to Moses, "This is what you must say to the people of Israel: Yahweh Elohim of your ancestors, the Elohim of Abraham, Isaac, and Jacob, has sent me to you. This is my name forever. This is my title throughout every generation."

WEB: Moses said to God, "Behold, when I come to the children of Israel, and tell them, 'The God of your fathers has sent me to you;' and they ask me, 'What is his name?' What should I tell them?" God said moreover to Moses, "You shall tell the children of Israel this, 'Yahweh, the God of your fathers, the God of Abraham, the God of Isaac, and the God of Jacob, has sent me to you.' This is my name forever, and this is my memorial to all generations."

Pastor Ken Hemphill writes: "Most Bible scholars would agree that the name Yahweh, or Jehovah, as it is sometimes translated, would be the proper name of God. The other names, including the compound names, provide further revelation of His character and His activity. JEHOVAH (YHWH…or JHVH) Note that the 4 letters (tetra means 4) of YHWH are often referred to as the Tetragrammaton. Vowels were added to the Tetragrammaton (literally "four lettered name"…Prior to 6th century Hebrew has no vowels—added to text AD 600-700) yielding the Name…YAHWEH … which is most commonly transliterated (transcribed from one alphabet into corresponding letters of another alphabet) as…JEHOVAH. Various scholars have suggested different translations of the name of God used in this passage. The name is from the imperfect stem of the Hebrew verb "to be." The imperfect tense denotes an action that started in the past, continues in the present, but is not yet complete. Many Bible scholars follow the simple translation that we have in our text, "I am who I am." One of our Old Testament scholars at Southwestern translates it this way: "I AM who I have always been." I like this translation because it affirms that the God who spoke from the burning bush is the same God who worked through the lives of Abraham, Isaac, and Jacob. It also implies His ability and desire to work through Moses in the present and the future. However we translate this name, we can be assured that it affirms God's self-existence and His eternality."

Pastor Alexander Maclaren writes in his Expositions of Holy Scripture: "The fire that burns and does not burn out, which has no tendency to destruction in its very energy, and is not consumed by its own activity, is surely a symbol of the One Being, whose being derives its law and its source from itself, who only can say—"I AM THAT I AM"—the law of His nature, the foundation of His being, the only conditions of His existence being, as it were, enclosed within the limits of His own nature. He says, "I AM THAT I AM." All other creatures are links; this is the staple from which they all hang. All other being is derived, and therefore limited and changeful; this being is underived, absolute, self-dependent, and therefore unalterable forevermore. Because we live, we die. In living, the process is going on of which death is the end. But God lives forevermore, a flame that does not burn out; therefore His resources are inexhaustible, His power unwearied. He needs no rest for recuperation of wasted energy. His gifts diminish not the store which He has to bestow. He gives and is none the poorer. He works and is never weary. He operates unspent; He loves and He loves forever. And through the ages, the fire burns on, unconsumed and un-decayed."

Pastor John Piper writes: "The most common and the most important name for God in the Old Testament is a name that in our English versions never even gets translated. Whenever you see the word LORD in all capital letters, you know that this name is behind it. In Hebrew the name had four letters — YHWH — and may have been pronounced something like Yahweh. The Jews came to regard this word with such reverence that they would never take it upon their lips, lest they inadvertently take the name in vain. So whenever they came to this name in their reading, they pronounced the word *"adonai"* which means "my lord." The English versions have basically followed the same pattern. They translate the proper name Yahweh with the word LORD in all caps. This approach is not a very satisfactory thing to do, because the English word LORD does not communicate to our ears a proper name like John or Michael or Noël. But Yahweh is God's proper name in Hebrew. The importance of it can be seen in the sheer frequency of its use. It occurs 6,828 times in the Old Testament. That's more than three times as often as the simple word for "God" (Elohim – 2,600; El – 238). What this fact shows is that God aims to be known not as a generic deity, but as a specific Person with a name that carries his unique character and mission. (Note: The word "Jehovah" originated from an attempt to pronounce the consonants YHWH with the vowels from the word *adonai*. In the oldest Hebrew texts there are no vowels. So it is easy to see how this would happen since whenever YHWH occurred in the text, the word adonai was pronounced by the reverent Jew.) The most important text in all the Bible for understanding the meaning of the name Yahweh is Exodus 3:13,15. God has just commanded Moses to go to Egypt and to bring his people Israel out of captivity. Moses says to God, "'If I come to the people of Israel and say to them, "The God of your fathers has sent me to you," and they ask me, "What is his name?" what shall I say to them?' God said to Moses, 'I AM WHO I AM.' And he said, 'Say this to the people of Israel, "I AM has sent me to you."' God also said to Moses, 'Say this to the people of Israel, "The LORD (that is, Yahweh!), the God of your fathers, the God of Abraham, the God of Isaac, the God of Jacob, has sent me to you." This is my name forever, and thus I am to be remembered throughout all generations.'" Two facts persuade me that this text provides an interpretation of the name Yahweh. One is that the name Yahweh and the name I AM are built out of the same Hebrew word *(hayah)*. The other is that Yahweh seems to be used here interchangeably with I AM. "I AM has sent me to you" (v. 14). "Yahweh…has sent me to you" (v. 15). I think it would be safe to say that God's purpose in this meeting with Moses is to reveal, as he never had before (Exodus 6:2), the meaning of his personal name, Yahweh. The key is in the phrase, I AM, and especially in the phrase, I AM WHO I AM. So here is where we ought to spend a lot of time meditating. What does it mean when you ask your God, Who are you? and he answers, I AM WHO I AM? I hope you can begin to feel how important these words are. There aren't any words more important than these. Any words that you think might be are important only because these words are true. The more you ponder them, the more awesome they become."

Our world has seen more change from 1900 to the present than in all history recorded before 1900, and things continue to accelerate rapidly. As time speeds by, measured not just in minutes or seconds but in nanoseconds (billionths of a second), everything changes. Technology changes so fast in our twenty-first-century world that we can barely keep up with the upgrades on our computers. Our bodies undergo the inevitable aging process, and we witness constant upheaval in the nations of the world. Material things change and deteriorate. The changes in the world do not change God one bit or thwart his plans. He's the same yesterday, today, and forever, and his love extends to the next generation and the next. Our security can't be found in any of the things in this ever-changing world. Instead, our security is in God and his promises.

Unchanging Lord Jesus, Yahweh, I praise You and worship You for Your love and faithfulness that extend from one generation to the next. Thank You that although our circumstances may change and the things around us pass away, You remain the same forever. Help me to find my security in your eternal sameness. Through all generations, even before you made the earth, You have been our dwelling place. You are God, without beginning or end. I am thankful that wherever I go, I don't have to feel insecure or anxious because You are there! Thank You for Your faithfulness and loving-kindness that follows me all the days of my life. In Your mighty Name Above All Names—Yahweh, we pray, amen.

Look Up—meditate on Exodus 3:13,15

Look In—as you meditate on Exodus 3:13,15 pray to see how you might apply it to your life.

Look Out—as you meditate on Exodus 3:13,15 pray to see how you might apply it to your relationships with others.

Notes

King of Zion

PSALM 9:11

Sing praises to the Lord, who dwells in Zion, and declare among the people what He has done.

Psalm 9:11

26 King of Zion

King of Zion from Psalm 9:11...

ERV: Sing praises to the Lord, who sits as King in Zion. Tell the nations about the great things he has done.

Expanded: Sing praises to the Lord who is king on Mount [dwells on] Zion [the location of the Temple]. Tell the nations [among the peoples] what he has done.

NCV: Sing praises to the Lord who is king on Mount Zion. Tell the nations what he has done.

Benson Commentary: "As the special residence of his glory is in heaven, so the special residence of his grace is in his church, of which Zion was a type: there he meets his people with his promises and graces, and there he expects they should meet him with their praises and services. Declare among the people his doings—Not only among the Israelites, but to the heathen nations, that they may also be brought to the knowledge and worship of the true God. Sing praises to the Lord—As the result of these views of his character, and at the remembrance of his doings. The heart of the psalmist is full of exultation and joy at the remembrance of the divine interposition, and he naturally breaks out into these strong expressions, calling on others to rejoice also. Which dwelleth in Zion—As Zion was the place where at this time the tabernacle was set up, and the worship of God was celebrated, it is spoken of as his dwelling-place. Declare among the people his doings—Make general and wide proclamation of what he has done; that is, make him known abroad, in his true character, that others may be brought also to put their trust in him, and to Praise him."

Pastor John Gill writes: "The psalmist having determined in the strength of grace to praise the Lord himself, and show forth all his marvelous works, and given his reasons for it, both with respect to himself in particular, and with respect to the people of God in general, here calls upon others to engage in the same work; the Lord is not only to be praised, which may be done by celebrating the perfections of his nature, and the works of his hands; by giving him thanks for mercies temporal and spiritual, and by living to his glory; but his praises are to be sung by a modulation of the voice in musical notes, as the word used signifies; where the same word is used of the singing of birds; and this is to be done by the saints jointly, in concert together, as Paul and Silas in prison sang the praises of God; and there is great reason why they should join together in this work, since they share the blessings of divine grace in common together. Jehovah, to whom praises are to be sung, is described as the inhabitant of Zion, the ark and tabernacle being there before the temple was built, which were symbols of the divine Presence. God by his essence and power is everywhere, he fills heaven and earth, and cannot be contained in either; his glorious presence is in heaven; his gracious presence is in his church and among his people; where they dwell he dwells, and where he dwells they dwell: hence the church is called by the same name as the Lord is here, the inhabitant of Zion; and this description of him points out the place where his praises are to be sung, in Zion; who are to sing them, the members of the church; and the reason why, because the Lord dwells in Zion; and is there a refuge for his people, and protects them."

What does it mean to trust the Lord, the King of Zion? It means looking to Him as the source of our security and putting our faith in the grace, love, power, and protection of God when the inevitable pressures of life come. It means knowing as the psalmist did that as the mountains surround and protect Zion, the city of Jerusalem, God himself surrounds and shields His people. When we trust the Lord, we don't have to focus on the wicked and what they are doing or might do to us. We don't have to rehash our own woes. Even though there are problems the size of mountains facing us, we can cry out to the Lord who created the mountains and is able to move them. As we sing praises to Him, and focus on Him and His truth, He will encourage our hearts and help us to tell the nations about the great things He has done!

Lord Jesus, King of Zion, I put my trust in You today. You are my security and protection, my shield, my fortress, and my hiding place, and I sing praises to You. When enemies surround me and troubles multiply, help me to remember that you are ever faithful and that you surround and protect me, both now and forever. Thank You for the free gift of salvation, that we are justified on the basis of Your finished work on the Cross. Thank You that, right now, we are under the completely sufficient imputed righteousness of Christ. Because we have placed our trust in the finished work of Jesus Christ, we are redeemed by Your precious blood. The threat of failure, judgment, and condemnation has been removed. Knowing that God's love for us and approval of us will never be determined by our performance is the most encouraging promise to which we cling—what great things You have done! In Your mighty Name Above All Names—King of Zion, we pray, amen.

Look Up—meditate on Psalm 9:11

Look In—as you meditate on Psalm 9:11 pray to see how you might apply it to your life.

Look Out—as you meditate on Psalm 9:11 pray to see how you might apply it to your relationships with others.

Bibliography

All Biblical research, references, and source material referred to in this devotional were from the online site: http://www.preceptaustin.org/ from January 1-26, 2016

Notes

About the Author

Meet Beth Willis Miller, M.Ed., contributing author of three books: *Under His Wings: Truths to Heal Adopted, Orphaned, and Waiting Children's Hearts; 21 Stories of Generosity: Real Stories to Inspire a Full Life (A Life of Generosity); A New Song: Glimpses of the Grace Journey (an anthology of essays, poems, stories and photos celebrating God's grace on life's journey);* and member of the Advanced Writers and Speakers Association. Beth has a Master's degree in Education, in curriculum, instruction, and supervision. She writes articles on a variety of topics to inspire and encourage others. Her expertise as a creative and critical thinking specialist is steeped in years of experience as a writer, presenter, educator and former Florida Department of Education State Consultant for Gifted Education. Seeing others' lives transformed by the truth of God's Word is her passion and purpose. She is married with two adult children, and two adorable grandsons.
Website: bethwillismiller.blogspot.com

About the Illustrator

Krista Hamrick creates art that celebrates. It all began at the age of three when Krista created a family portrait of jellybean shaped people that had smiles connecting from eye to eye. Home was a secure, cozy and creative place, and as a painfully shy child, her favorite thing to do was to stay close to the nest and draw pictures. Art became a way for Krista to express herself without being the center of attention. Over the years, Krista's art has become more and more expressive of the faith and values that have shaped her as a person. Today, Krista is married with two teenage sons. Still introspective and eternally optimistic, she hopes to inspire you through her illustrations to celebrate your own life, gifts and relationships as well.
Website: kristahamrick.com

Made in the USA
Lexington, KY
26 June 2016